IMAGES
of America

DEARBORN INN

Airplanes coming and going from the Ford Airport were common in Dearborn at the time this photograph was taken in 1931. With the stately Dearborn Inn situated across the street from the airport terminal, it was conveniently located for travelers, who were welcome to watch air traffic from a promenade on the roof of the hotel. (Courtesy of The Henry Ford, THF23890.)

ON THE COVER: The graceful semicircular front driveway to Dearborn Inn still greets guests today, similar to how it appears in this 1931 photograph. It is not surprising to see Ford automobiles parked in front of this Ford hotel, which was situated across the street from the Ford Airport. One of the inn's signature lampposts is visible along the curb. (Courtesy of Walter P. Reuther Library, Wayne State University.)

IMAGES
of America

DEARBORN INN

*To Nancy —
With fond memories
from the Dearborn Inn.
Enjoy!*

Jennifer Czerwick Ganem

ARCADIA
PUBLISHING

Published by Arcadia Publishing
Charleston, South Carolina

Printed in the United States of America

Library of Congress Control Number: 2011929296

For all general information, please contact Arcadia Publishing:
Telephone 843-853-2070
Fax 843-853-0044
E-mail sales@arcadiapublishing.com
For customer service and orders:
Toll-Free 1-888-313-2665

Visit us on the Internet at www.arcadiapublishing.com

To my parents, Marlene and Henry Czerwick, and my family, Paul, Alysandra, and Andrew Ganem, with love

CONTENTS

Acknowledgments

Researching the history of Dearborn Inn has brought forth some of the most interesting pieces of information, amazing photographs, and incredible people, as well as a fascinating jigsaw puzzle of details; it has been a thoroughly enjoyable experience. The hospitality industry has proven that those in its employ are hospitable individuals themselves, and it is difficult to imagine writing a book about anything associated with so many friendly people as the Dearborn Inn.

My father, Henry Czerwick, has been a tremendous resource in extracting information from his extensive Ford history collection. His insights have only been surpassed by the Benson Ford Research Center at The Henry Ford and the highly professional staff of archivists and assistants who have been invaluable to this research on Dearborn Inn. Particular thanks go to Linda Skolarus and those who brought out countless boxes of materials for me to review.

Thanks go to the many librarians and archivists who preserved information over the years and assisted me at the following locations: Bentley Historical Library at the University of Michigan, Henry Ford Centennial Library, Walter P. Reuther Library and Wayne State University, Ford Motor Company, and Dearborn Historical Museum. For their kindness and generosity in supporting this project, special thanks also go to Adrian deVogel and family and to the family of Paul LeVeque.

It is not possible for me to avoid thanking Bob Pierce and the thousands of other employees, who have been the special caretakers of Dearborn Inn for over 80 years. This amazing hotel is a tribute to your dedication as stewards of a most important historical treasure.

Special appreciation needs to be extended to my family for their encouragement and help, as well as my many friends who have shared this Dearborn Inn research journey.

It is hard to believe that a Saturday afternoon phone call from a friend attending an antique market would result in a book, but here it is. My final thank you goes to Susan McCabe; thanks for the call and for your endless support. Your china is beautiful.

Unless otherwise noted, all images appear courtesy of the author.

INTRODUCTION

The Oakwood Hotel Company was established as the corporate entity to own Dearborn Inn, and on February 13, 1931, the State of Michigan issued articles of association to commence business. The first board of directors meeting took place on February 16, 1931, at 6:00 p.m. in the Buhl Building in Detroit, Michigan. Three directors were present: Richard S. DeCoursey, Wallace Visscher, and John W. Kiskadden. Once the meeting commenced and officers were elected, each of these men promptly tendered their resignations. The names of Ford employees B.J. Craig and William B. Mayo, along with Henry Ford's only son, Edsel B. Ford, were then brought forward to be directors. Minutes from this meeting reflect that the corporation had been deeded the following parcel of land, situated on Oakwood Boulevard in Wayne County, Michigan, described as:

> Beginning at the intersection of Oakwood Boulevard and Pelham Road thence running N.W. a distance of 791 feet, thence S.W. a distance of 748 feet, thence S.E. 749 feet to Pelham Road, then N.E. 790 feet to the place of beginning, containing 13.6 acres of land together with hotel building and garage nearing completion.

The original directors were subscribers for stock in the corporation. With their resignations, they assigned 1,000 shares of stock, at a par value of $100 per share, to the Ford Motor Company, except for three shares that would be issued to Craig, Mayo, and Edsel Ford. The corporation accepted the conveyance of real estate and agreed to pay Ford Motor Company an amount to be determined as the fair value of the land, together with the cost to Ford Motor Company for buildings and other improvements. It was noted that Ford Motor Company would set up a liability on their books equal to the fair value of land, plus cost of improvements, less $100,000 represented by the shares of stock issued.

As president and chairman, Edsel Ford then presented the other officers a contract between Oakwood Hotel Company and L.G. Treadway Service Corporation, a New York corporation, for the operation of this hotel, garage, and other properties. An inn was about to open.

L.G. Treadway was already managing Wayside Inn in Sudsbury, Massachusetts, which was owned by Ford, and this firm would provide similar services for Ford's Botsford Inn in Farmington, Michigan. The arrangement would remain intact until April 1939, when Oakwood Hotel Company would dissolve, selling the assets of Dearborn Inn and Botsford Inn for $1,426,313 to Seaboard Properties Company, a Delaware corporation owned by Ford Motor Company. The Seaboard Investment Company was organized for the purpose of taking over certain assets of the Dutee Wilcox Flint properties in New England and held considerable bank stock. Seaboard acquired the White Hart Inn in Salisbury, Connecticut, for just under $55,000, which was frequented by the Edsel Ford family while their sons attended nearby private Hotchkiss School, and Seaboard went on to oversee the Dearborn Country Club, too.

Ford employees H.L. Moekle, B.J. Craig, and John Crawford served as the initial directors of Seaboard. Due to all of the stock being owned by Ford Motor Company, the directors quickly proposed that a new board be seated with Henry Ford, Edsel B. Ford, and P.E. Martin as officers and with the recommendation to consider Henry Ford II as a possible board member as well. Years later, William Clay Ford ultimately became a chairman of Seaboard, which was gifted to the Edison Institute in 1953 to provide added revenue for the Henry Ford Museum and Greenfield

Village (now known as The Henry Ford). The Edison Institute officially dissolved Seaboard in July 1983.

In more than 80 years of operation, the hotel has never been far from some aspect of Ford oversight. Still in operation today for all to enjoy, Dearborn Inn is owned by Ford Land Development and is operated by Marriott International.

One

DEARBORN, FORD,

AND AIRPLANES

The city of Dearborn is now a community of nearly 100,000 residents, but it is a town that came from humble beginnings. Heavily overgrown and wooded, traveled by early Native Americans, and first settled by adventurous Europeans in 1786, this once wilderness area of southeast Michigan was established as the village of Dearborn in 1836, and in 1863 Dearborn became the birthplace and ultimate home of one of the world's most famous industrialists, Henry Ford.

Although well known for his founding of the Ford Motor Company, his 1914 announcement to pay workers $5 a day, his innovation of the assembly line, and his contributions to "putting the world on wheels," Henry Ford had many far-reaching interests and hobbies that left a much broader legacy than just his famous Model T and advancements in the automotive world.

If nothing else, Henry Ford was a visionary, and he possessed the wealth to support his interests. In the 1920s, his son, Edsel, would encourage his involvement with aviation, and soon the Ford Airport would be constructed in Dearborn. Even earlier, Ford had begun collecting Americana for a museum and village that he was building in Dearborn. And on October 21, 1929, the eyes of the world were on Dearborn as Ford hosted a celebration of his friend Thomas Edison, commemorating the 50th anniversary of the incandescent lamp during the Light's Golden Jubilee. Ford had already begun to change Dearborn forever.

During the 1920s, the Ford name became associated with aviation and the National Air Tour, a series of annual aerial tours sponsored in part by Ford from 1925 to 1931, with the top prize including the Edsel B. Ford Reliability Trophy. As more passengers and pilots came and went from the Ford Airport, and as Dearborn greeted dignitaries such as President Hoover, Orville Wright, John D. Rockefeller Jr., and Madame Curie, Henry Ford came to appreciate that the town needed a full-service hotel in closer proximity than Detroit.

The Ford Airport was already boasting many firsts—first paved runway, first US Airmail route, and first radio signal—and Edsel Ford had seen to it that everything about the airport would be of modern design. However, when the need for a hotel arose to accommodate pilots, passengers, and other visitors to Dearborn, it was Henry Ford that chose the traditional, Georgian-style architecture and charming appointments of a New England inn for the structure that would become the Dearborn Inn.

As a touch of Ford grandeur was put forth in the building of the 108-room hotel, which would be filled with early-American furnishings, Henry Ford made it clear that the inn was not being built to be a profit-making venture, but rather to host visitors to Dearborn, including the Ford Tractor Plant, Ford Engineering Laboratory, and the Edison Institute, and to illustrate his idea of what a modern hotel should be.

Opening its doors on July 1, 1931, and still in operation today, Dearborn Inn went on into the record books with many firsts of its own. Designated as both a national and Michigan state historic site, the inn still possesses the splendor that Ford envisioned when hiring noted architect Albert Kahn to design the hotel. And throughout the years, as multimillion-dollar renovations have brought updates to the facility, great care has been taken to preserve the character and integrity Ford originally created.

Dearborn Inn has always been more than just a hotel, and through its doors has gone many famous individuals, including Eleanor Roosevelt, Norman Rockwell, Charles Lindbergh, George Washington Carver, Ronald Reagan, and even Lassie. The addition of five architecturally correct historic cottages replicating the homes of famous Americans Patrick Henry, Walt Whitman, Barbara Fritchie, Edgar Allan Poe, and Oliver Wolcott created a Colonial Village like none other, with each building still available for guest use when choosing to stay at Dearborn Inn.

From Detroit, to Highland Park, to Dearborn, and to far reaching places around the world, Henry Ford accomplished amazing things, touching the lives of millions and changing the world forever. The Dearborn Inn is one more fascinating chapter in the incredible Ford story.

Engineering Laboratory and Airport
Ford Motor Company

The Ford Airport Terminal Building was not constructed when this photograph was taken, but the Ford Engineering Laboratory can be seen in the foreground. The land in the background is the Ford Motor Company test track today, but it was previously used by Ford as an airport. Land in the upper right of this image is where Dearborn Inn was eventually constructed. (Courtesy of Henry Czerwick.)

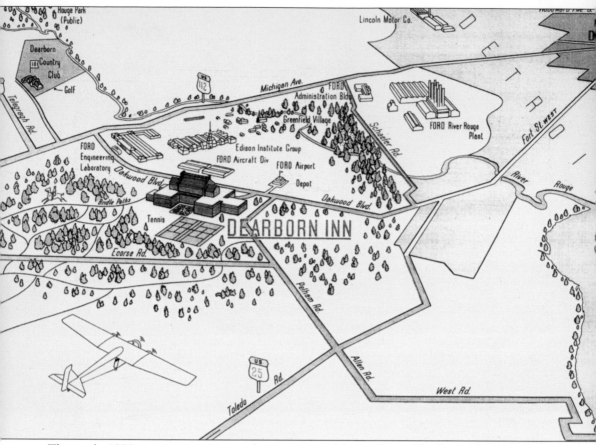

This early-1930s map approximates the positions of "most things Ford" in relation to major roadways around Dearborn. Dearborn Inn is prominently depicted in the center of the illustration, directly across from the Ford Airport, while the Ford Rouge Plant, Ford Administration Building, Dearborn Country Club, Ford Engineering Laboratory, Edison Institute, and Greenfield Village are also indicated. This map shows how Allen Road becomes Pelham Road, traveling right through to Oakwood Boulevard alongside the inn. Note the airplane in the foreground that is heading in for a landing. (Courtesy of Henry Ford Centennial Library.)

It is Edsel Ford who is attributed with drawing Henry Ford's interests toward aviation, and father and son were regularly involved with activities at the Ford Airport. Ford was the first private carrier to fly US Airmail, which helped to demonstrate that scheduled air service could be reliable. In January 1926, Ford was awarded contracts from the postal service for the Detroit to Chicago and Detroit to Cleveland mail routes. Pictured in front of a Ford Tri-Motor airplane, Edsel (center) is holding a hat and talking with William B. Stout, while Henry is to the far right. (Courtesy of Walter P. Reuther Library, Wayne State University.)

The Ford Airport and airfield are pictured here, with the clock tower of the Henry Ford Museum visible along the very top edge of the photograph. Oakwood Boulevard runs vertically through the photograph, and the perpendicular road on the left edge is Pelham Road. Located on the property that will become the front lawn of Dearborn Inn, cars are parked across the street from the Ford Airport and terminal. (Courtesy of Walter P. Reuther Library, Wayne State University.)

Crowds gathered in great numbers to witness the National Air Tour and air shows at the Ford Airport. Shown here is Henry Ford alongside Charles Lindbergh, who is getting ready to board this Ford Flivver airplane. (Courtesy of Walter P. Reuther Library, Wayne State University.)

This view of the Ford Airport was taken from the roof of Dearborn Inn, where guests were welcome to observe air traffic from a promenade. The image is of the Edsel B. Ford Reliability Tour, which occurred just two weeks after the hotel opened and marked the last of the National Air Tours that took place at the Ford Airport. (Courtesy of The Henry Ford, THF23889.)

THE FORD AIRPORT

At this airport, built by Henry Ford in 1924, world and national aviation history was made, ushering in a new era of flight embracing the all-metal airliner, radio control devices, air mail, scheduled flights, and the airline services that the generation of the 1930's came to expect.

For the first time in the world:
A hotel, the Dearborn Inn, was designed and built for the air traveler.
A guided flight of a commercial airliner was made by radio.

For the first time in the U. S. A.:
An all-metal, multi-engine, commercial airliner was built.
A regularly scheduled passenger airline in continuous domestic service was inaugurated.
Under the Kelly Act the first contract air mail for domestic routes was flown.
An airline terminal for passenger use was constructed.

The airport's closing in 1933 ended Ford's experimental work in aviation.

This Michigan State Historic Site Marker (No.126) sits in front of Dearborn Inn and is directly across from the former the Ford Airport. It states the following: "At this airport, built by Henry Ford in 1924, world and national aviation history was made, ushering in a new era of flight embracing the all-metal airliner, radio control devices, airmail, scheduled flights, and the airline services that the generation of the 1930s came to expect. For the first time in the world: A hotel, the Dearborn Inn, was designed for the air traveler. A guided flight of a commercial airliner was made by radio. For the first time in the U.S.A.: An all-metal, multi-engine, commercial airliner was built. A regularly scheduled passenger airline in continuous domestic service was inaugurated. Under the Kelly Act the first contract airmail for domestic routes was flown. An airline terminal for passenger use was constructed. The airport's closing in 1933 ended Ford's experimental work in aviation."

The mooring mast at the Ford Airport was a Dearborn landmark for many years; this postcard also shows the airfield and hangar.

In 1931, this US Navy vessel docked on the mooring mast at the Ford Airport. The enormous dirigible was quite a sight and drew a sizable crowd.

DEARBORN INN

This is one of the earliest photographs of the completed inn in the early 1930s. In the book, *The Aviation Legacy of Henry and Edsel Ford* by Tim O'Callaghan, the author reveals that it was in the October 1931 issue of *Aero Digest* that Dearborn Inn was described as being "probably the first modern hotel to be located adjacent to an airport." Throughout the years, Dearborn Inn was promoted as the world's first airport hotel, and it has certainly distinguished itself as a one-of-a-kind establishment. However, historians have designated the 37-room Oakland Airport Inn in California as an earlier airport hotel, having opened in 1929, followed by a short list of other aviation-based hostelries that were operating prior to Dearborn Inn—though none likely as modern as Ford's airport hotel.

Henry Ford was not concerned about the inn turning a profit, which was a good thing since it opened during the Great Depression. However, there are plenty of memos from the Ford auditing department addressing costs, staffing, delinquent accounts, opportunities for efficiencies, and overall losses, which went on for years. The first month of operation, the inn lost $7,463; one year later, losses for the month of July 1932 were $1,067.

Eventually, the property surrounding the inn was increased to approximately 24 acres, and the large expanse of lush lawn in front of the hotel has remained the lovely foreground for the stately inn. In October 1971, the front lawn of Dearborn Inn was the first Dearborn location entered in a national directory for being a "helistop" for helicopters, a great tribute to the inn's aviation history.

THE UNITED STATES DEPARTMENT OF INTERIOR HAS PLACED THIS PROPERTY ON THE NATIONAL REGISTER OF HISTORIC PLACES

Dearborn Inn has been distinguished in many ways. In May 1983, this plaque was mounted on the front of the inn to designate the property as being listed in the National Register of Historic Places.

Two

BUILD IT,
AND THEY WILL COME

"Henry Ford Builds Modern Hotel" was the headline in the September 1930 issue of *The Dearbornite* magazine. The article explained:

> Just opposite the Ford Airport and situated 300 feet back from Oakwood Boulevard, Henry Ford is erecting a building that is of vital interest to all Dearborn. . . . Contracts for construction have been awarded and work is going forward rapidly. The entire exterior of the building is to be of American Colonial design to harmonize with the [Henry Ford] Museum. The lobby, a large and dignified room of colonial precedent, is approached through an arcaded loggia extending across the entire front of the main building between two extending wings.

When the doors to Dearborn Inn opened on July 1, 1931, patrons had an amazing view of Ford Airport from the roof of the hotel or from the wide, arched windows of the main dining room. But Ford's interests in flight would not go on much longer, and the country was in the midst of the Great Depression. Yet, something so special was created within the walls of this hostelry that even now, over 80 years later, Dearborn Inn continues to flourish as a hotel, currently operated by Marriott International.

The inn has been boasted as the world's first airport hotel, but that claim has been clearly challenged. However, it is noted for many other firsts, like the first air-conditioned hotel (installed in 1934), the first to recreate replicas of great American homes for use as guest cottages, the first to pioneer a guest-room telephone system, and the first hotel to have exhibit/banquet space with drive-in access for vehicles.

Once open, Dearborn Inn was touted as having "excellent accommodations, not only to business visitors arriving daily at the Ford Motor Company's plant and the Ford Airport, but also to thousands of visitors who come to see Greenfield Village and the Edison Institute of Technology, as well as visitors to the Ford Engineering Laboratories," the *Dearborn Independent* newspaper reported just two days after the inn opened.

Dearborn Inn extended its hospitality to dignitaries and celebrities. "Scarcely a day goes by," said inn manager Richard McLain in a 1958 *Dearborn Guide* newspaper interview, "that we do not have someone come in who is in the public eye. Only this morning, former Governor of New Jersey Charles Edison (son of Thomas Edison) and Sir Patrick Hennessey, chairman of the board of England's Ford Motor Company, were here." But Dearborn Inn would also be the backdrop for thousands of other special occasions for local families, including weddings, graduations, birthdays, anniversaries, and holiday celebrations.

In an article titled "Decorative Dancing and Damask Dining," written by Tara B. Gnau for the 1981 summer issue of *The Dearborn Historian*, the author describes the early years of Dearborn Inn being "a magnet for Dearborn's social life." The article states that the "1930s newspaper advertisements include 'Dearborn Inn Chatter' listing club meetings, special dances, and guests, as well as the 'Musicale.' Many vocal and instrumental groups and soloists performed at the Inn in concert for the guests and general public." The employees were known to have formed a weekly social club amongst themselves as well.

So much history would lie ahead, but first, Dearborn Inn would need to be built.

The Martin Krausmann Company was the general contractor of this building designed by Albert Kahn and Associates. On the first day of construction, June 30, 1930, this was the crew and equipment assigned to begin the site preparation. Something magnificent was about to happen. (Courtesy of Bentley Historical Library, University of Michigan, Albert Kahn Dearborn Inn, Box 10, Folder 1504.)

On July 1, 1930, the site of Dearborn Inn was little more than an empty field. Yet, the doors of the new hotel would open one year from the day this picture was taken. Much would be accomplished in the next 365 days. (Courtesy of Bentley Historical Library, University of Michigan.)

"Ford Airport Hotel Construction Begins" was a small headline appearing on the front page of the August 1, 1930, edition of the *Dearborn Independent* newspaper. "New Three-Story Structure Will Be Completed Early Next Year" was the following sub-headline. "Ford Motor Co. Hotel Building" was another name given to the construction project that would become known as Dearborn Inn. (Courtesy of Bentley Historical Library, University of Michigan.)

The beautifully landscaped property and lush lawns associated with Dearborn Inn started as this weed-covered field, which was once one of many family-owned farms in Dearborn. (Courtesy of Bentley Historical Library, University of Michigan.)

The footings to Dearborn Inn look like a complex maze. Years later, when the inn would undergo major renovations from 1987 to 1989, a representative from the contracting firm of John M. Olsen would comment on the massive foundation as being "similar to those that you would find in an industrial type of building." (Courtesy of Bentley Historical Library, University of Michigan.)

This image certainly depicts the enormity of what was involved with the site preparation, groundwork, and footings from which Dearborn Inn would rise. This view was taken from the rear of the hotel, and traffic in the background is located on Oakwood Boulevard. Somewhat obscured behind the construction in the center is the terminal for the Ford Airport. A good-sized crew of men works quickly on the construction site, while lumber is strewn throughout the area. What appears to be a paint can in the foreground must have been used to carry something else, since painting had yet to take place. (Courtesy of Bentley Historical Library, University of Michigan.)

A series of planks in the foreground has been laid to make a wooden sidewalk for workmen, and other timber has been laid end to end to create temporary walkways. The wheelbarrow tipped on its side is a reminder of how much manual labor was taking place. A stack of bricks has been delivered to the construction site, and bricklayers are beginning to build the walls at two corners. (Courtesy of Bentley Historical Library, University of Michigan.)

"Construction work has begun on the new Ford hotel, being erected by Henry Ford on a site directly across from the Ford airport terminal of the Stout Air Lines on Oakwood Boulevard," reported the August 1930 *Dearborn Independent*. It went on to state, "The site, which was surveyed some weeks ago, is located about 200 feet south of the highway. For background it has a group of tall trees and for foreground, when completed, will have a wide, landscaped lawn." This picture was taken August 11, 1930, about six weeks into construction. In the background is a structure serving as the construction office; this building would be removed from the premises before the inn opened. (Courtesy of Bentley Historical Library, University of Michigan.)

This September 8, 1930, image shows the construction site with the basic foundation in place. The scene is lacking of any major heavy construction equipment. Of note are the many arched windows that are in place, with brickwork beginning to give the hotel its distinct architectural design. (Courtesy of Bentley Historical Library, University of Michigan.)

While a good deal of brickwork has taken place to the wings of the building, the steel framework for the main portion of the inn has risen, creating the skeleton that would shape this marvelous structure. "The entire exterior of the building is of American colonial design to harmonize with the Ford museum nearby," stated the *Dearborn Independent* a year before the hotel would open. (Courtesy of Bentley Historical Library, University of Michigan.)

Two photographs were taken side by side to create a panoramic image of the rear of the hotel, looking in toward the center of the courtyard, with the soon-to-be garage to the left. (Courtesy

of Bentley Historical Library, University of Michigan.)

Three months into the construction process, the stately details of Dearborn Inn really started to take shape. Here, supplies are stacked high in front of the hotel. (Courtesy of Bentley Historical Library, University of Michigan.)

This first glimpse inside the inn shows scaffolding and ladders, with just a couple of workmen in view. (Courtesy of Bentley Historical Library, University of Michigan.)

A view from behind the inn shows the wide opening for the garage door, as well as the three tall, graceful arches that will lead to the porch from the courtyard. A long chute can be seen coming from a second-floor window, allowing for construction debris to be safely removed. (Courtesy of Bentley Historical Library, University of Michigan.)

Winter is approaching quickly, and this November 1930 photograph shares the story that the main roof is not yet complete. However, the walls are up, and the windows are boarded. (Courtesy of Bentley Historical Library, University of Michigan.)

This interior view of ductwork, as well as a couple of busy workmen, is believed to be an area near the elevator shaft. (Courtesy of Bentley Historical Library, University of Michigan.)

Cold weather likely served as an incentive to keep construction moving quickly, because by November 28, 1930, the roof had been placed on the main building—just in time for the arrival of snow. (Courtesy of Bentley Historical Library, University of Michigan.)

An observation deck on the roof was designed to allow guests a good view of airplanes arriving and departing from the Ford Airport across the street. This November 28, 1930, view of the roof shows boarded windows and a light covering of snow. (Courtesy of Bentley Historical Library, University of Michigan.)

In the lobby on the main floor, construction materials are stacked in piles. In the center of the image is the fireplace brickwork underway. To the right of the fireplace is a glimpse far back into the space that would become the formal dining area, which was to be known as the Early American Room. (Courtesy of Bentley Historical Library, University of Michigan.)

Here, Dearborn Inn is set to open its doors in less than seven months, but inside there is still so much construction work underway. (Courtesy of Bentley Historical Library, University of Michigan.)

Still under construction, this interior view of the Dearborn Inn garage shows that the drive-thru doors have been installed. (Courtesy of Bentley Historical Library, University of Michigan.)

In this image of the rear of the hotel, the garage doors can be seen. A temporary building has been erected in the courtyard, likely serving as the construction office during cold-weather months. (Courtesy of Bentley Historical Library, University of Michigan.)

This scaffolding in the interior of the building served to elevate workers closer to the ceiling. (Courtesy of Bentley Historical Library, University of Michigan.)

Very little work appears to be taking place outdoors during this phase of the project. The windows are boarded over, and while the roof is on, shingles are still not in place. (Courtesy of Bentley Historical Library, University of Michigan.)

By mid-January, work continued on the interior of the structure. In just a few weeks, on February 13, 1931, the State of Michigan would issue articles of association to the Oakwood Hotel Company to commence business. (Courtesy of Bentley Historical Library, University of Michigan.)

As the beautiful inn was under construction, Ford made arrangements for the L.G. Treadway Service Corporation of New York City to furnish, equip, and operate the hotel with its 108 guest rooms. The original staff was brought in from New England, with Charles E. Graham as the first manager. (Courtesy of Bentley Historical Library, University of Michigan.)

In March, some exterior landscaping was underway, with large trees having been transplanted to the front lawn. (Courtesy of Bentley Historical Library, University of Michigan.)

By March 9, 1931, work was well underway on the interior of the structure. This somewhat unbelievable scene of the main lobby shares a view of the mess involved in creating what was to become an exceedingly elegant room. A trough of wet plaster is seen in the foreground, as well as barrels, shovels, and bags of plaster supplies. Although the ceiling appears to be finished, temporary electric lines have been strung to provide light. A clock can be seen hung on the rear wall over the doorway entrance to the front desk. The door on the far left leads to the front of the inn. (Courtesy of Bentley Historical Library, University of Michigan.)

This image of a corridor on an upper floor was taken on March 17, 1931, and shows plasterwork well underway. Much finishing work, wiring, and flooring are yet to be completed. (Courtesy of Bentley Historical Library, University of Michigan.)

On the same floor, this area near the elevator has also been plastered, with much detail work still needed. (Courtesy of Bentley Historical Library, University of Michigan.)

The ductwork gives a behind-the-scenes perspective of the complexity of the engineering work that went into the design of Dearborn Inn. Albert Kahn and Associates handled all of this planning, already having a long and successful relationship with Ford. (Courtesy of Bentley Historical Library, University of Michigan.)

The interior of the hotel was being accurately described in August 1930, as the *Dearborn Independent* reported, "At one end of the lobby will be the hotel office, porter, check room, elevators, and entrance to the guest rooms. At the other will be the main dining room, the windows of which will overlook the airport." (Courtesy of Bentley Historical Library, University of Michigan.)

The boiler room of the Dearborn Inn is shown here still under construction, but the space would go on to be painted and spotlessly clean as Henry Ford would expect. (Courtesy of Bentley Historical Library, University of Michigan.)

Gleaming is the best word to describe the freshly painted interior of the garage. This space would later be renovated into the Greenfield Banquet Hall. Today, this area of the hotel houses administrative offices. (Courtesy of Bentley Historical Library, University of Michigan.)

By the end of April 1931, landscaping was in place, and the distinctive semicircular front driveway was taking shape. Here, several men are overseeing aspects of the curb work and gravel foundation. The deep hole toward the left foreground may have been used in preparing the installation of one of the distinctive lamp fixtures that would later grace both sides of the driveway. (Courtesy of Bentley Historical Library, University of Michigan.)

Managing the supplies and construction materials was a major task. Here, sawhorses, bricks, and lumber are gathered. At this time, opening day was less than three months away. (Courtesy of Bentley Historical Library, University of Michigan.)

When the inn opened in July, the *Dearborn Independent* explained, "There also is an observation roof which permits the guest an opportunity of seeing the planes take off and land," which was located adjacent to the Ford Airport. This is a view from May 1931. (Courtesy of Bentley Historical Library, University of Michigan.)

With less than one month before the inn was to open, this scene of the hotel's kitchen provides a glimpse of the frenzy taking place as the grand opening date approached. Workmen have hung up their jackets, and in the foreground their toolboxes are wide open on the floor. A leather bag is perched on an unopened wooden crate marked, "THIS END UP." The wall tiles have been grouted, but an empty hole on the central pillar, as well as wires dangling from the ceiling, indicate some unfinished work in this area. (Courtesy of Bentley Historical Library, University of Michigan.)

A workman can be seen on his knees in this photograph, with a metal lunch box and insulated coffee bottle nearby on a counter. Crates fill the room, including one containing a Crescent Electric Dish and Glasswasher, a product of the Hobart Manufacturing Co. of Troy, Ohio. The same crate also promotes Hobart as making mixers, coffee mills, potato peelers, meat choppers, food cutters, and slicing machines. (Courtesy of Bentley Historical Library, University of Michigan.)

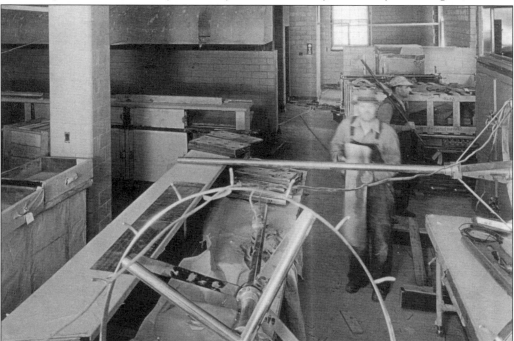

The kitchen served the inn well and served guests amazing and memorable meals. On April 8, 1949, a fire raged in this kitchen "for approximately ten minutes with a series of explosions which shook the building from end to end," reported Robert Hamilton, manager of the inn, to Seaboard Properties and to B.J. Craig in a letter assessing the damage. (Courtesy of Bentley Historical Library, University of Michigan.)

The Colonial Lounge was a parlor designed for guests to relax. On June 9, 1931, with the inn scheduled to open in just a few weeks, this photograph shows ladders in view and the doors leading out toward the front of the inn still off the hinges and leaning against the wall. Clara Ford hosted friends for tea in this room. In 1949, two years after Henry Ford's death, the room was remodeled for use as a cocktail lounge. In later years, local businessmen referred to the buffet lunch served here as the "fat man's club." (Courtesy of Bentley Historical Library, University of Michigan.)

This photograph depicts the kitchen, as well as the coffee shop. Two horseshoe-shaped counters were originally installed in the Old English Coffee Shop, and workmen can be seen putting on some finishing touches. (Courtesy of Bentley Historical Library, University of Michigan.)

This image was taken from an interesting angle behind the inn and shows the roadway leading to the garage (far right). The land in the distance was later developed by Ford Motor Company. (Courtesy of Bentley Historical Library, University of Michigan.)

Three

GREETINGS FROM THE DEARBORN INN

From the very beginning, Dearborn Inn set itself apart as an extraordinary place, and people took note. In a May 1932 article written by James Marsdale in the magazine *Building Maintenance*, the headline "Scrupulous Cleanliness is the Dominating Factor" perfectly described the inn. The article went on as follows:

> The story is told of a woman, herself a meticulous housewife, who once was one of the thousands of persons who visit the Ford Motor Company throughout the year. The good woman had progressed through the immaculate corridors and departments of several buildings and at the end of the trip had only one remark to make. With perhaps typical feminine and jealous "touchiness" she said, "I think Mr. Ford is a crank on cleanliness."
>
> Add that to his virtues or his debits as you prefer; Mr. Ford IS a crank on cleanliness. And if you want proof of this just drive around the curve of Oakwood Boulevard or set your plane down at the Ford Airport at Dearborn, Michigan, and step in at the Dearborn Inn which is hard by.
>
> The Dearborn Inn stands in a delightful setting of 13 acres of lawns, gardens, and woods opposite the Ford properties including the laboratory, airport, and the now famous "Greenfield Village." Recognized as the finest construction of its kind in the world, it is of stately Georgian architecture that seems to welcome the traveler.
>
> When you enter Dearborn Inn you are charmed with its comfortable and spacious interior furnished in perfect reproductions of early American pieces in pine, maple, and mahogany. If you are to be an overnight guest you are equally pleased with your room—one of 108 bedrooms, beautifully furnished and equipped with luxurious appointments including private bath and shower, radio and electric clock, circulating ice water, and every other desired convenience.
>
> Later you will visit the dining room or coffee shop and may note the tasteful furnishings and the brightness of equipment, Allegheny steel being used for all metal parts. Finally you may sit at ease in the lounge or step down to the well-equipped basement recreation room.

Throughout your inspection there has been a sense of super-something about the place. Then it "comes" to you: It's the supreme cleanliness. The work of the diligent Ford housekeeping hand is visible. The place was built by Mr. Ford and is under his general supervision. It is operated by the capable L.G. Treadway Service Corporation under the management of Mr. C.E. Graham. Here indeed is a building that might have been featured in the "Spotless Town" advertising of an earlier day.

Throughout the years, tremendous effort has been put forth in maintaining Dearborn Inn and preserving its many architectural details. During a major renovation that took place during the late 1980s, a team of inspectors from the National Historic Trust visited the property about every six months to make certain that the feel and ambience of the inn was being maintained and to assure the hotel would be eligible to retain its listing in the National Historic Register. Special attention was given to refinishing trim, recreating plaster moldings, and restoring original guest-room windows to operating order.

As countless numbers of guests have visited Dearborn Inn throughout the years, they have been met by a team of dedicated caretakers that has worked diligently to maintain a magnificent historic treasure for future generations. Henry Ford would be proud.

Invitations were sent, and the local headlines reported, "Gay Reception Marks Dearborn Inn Opening: One Thousand, Including State's Great, Attend Open House at New Ford Hotel." According to the July 3, 1931, edition of the *Dearborn Independent*, "This city's new colonial hotel recently erected by Henry Ford at Oakwood Boulevard, across from the Ford airport, at a cost of $500,000, was officially opened at an open-house reception Wednesday afternoon that included several of Michigan's leading citizens." The guest book reveals many distinguished attendees on July 1, 1931, including Mr. Henry and Mrs. Clara Ford, Mr. Edsel and Mrs. Eleanor Ford, and Gov. and Mrs. Clara M. Bruckner, as well as Detroit mayor Frank Murphy, Dearborn mayor Clyde Ford, Mr. and Mrs. M. Himelhoch, and Mr. and Mrs. Robert A. Oakman. (Courtesy of the Dearborn Historical Museum.)

Those familiar with Dearborn today would have difficulty imagining an area of winding road one mile from Dearborn Inn looking anything like this scene. This classic roadside sign features a watchman pointing the way just "one mile to the Dearborn Inn." Based on old advertising literature providing directions to the inn, this sign was likely located on Pelham Road. It was photographed within a month of the hotel opening in July 1931. (Courtesy of The Henry Ford, Acc. 1660, Box 121, 833-56316-2.)

"The Inn has been described by hotel architects as the most perfect hotel structure of its type in the United States," the *Dearborn Independent* reported. It went on to state, "The grounds have been beautifully gardened, the effect being more that of natural beauty than cultivated." In this photograph, the tall trees in front of the inn are being secured to the ground with roping, having recently been transplanted, despite their size. (Courtesy of Walter P. Reuther Library, Wayne State University.)

Outstanding details of the rear of the inn can be seen here, and the wing to the far right includes rooms in "Pilot's Row" on the first floor. The courtyard is clearly visible and landscaped with a tree in the center, which is the same location as the construction office that sat there just months earlier. A car can be viewed driving toward the inn's garage, and because there is an added floor above the garage, this picture was taken after the 1932 Alexandria Ballroom addition. The photograph also clearly shows the location of the tennis courts and children's playground. The word "FORD" can be spotted on the airfield at the top of the image; guests who enjoyed the rooftop observation deck clearly had a great view of air traffic. (Courtesy of The Henry Ford, Acc. 1660, Box 121, 121-7, 63669-D.)

This aerial view provides a visual layout of the inn and its distinctive semicircular driveway in relation to the Ford Airport terminal located across the street. Beneath the photographer's airplane, another airplane has been captured in flight and is found in the center of the image. The addition of the Alexandria Ballroom also dates this photograph as 1932 or later. There are many cars parked along Oakwood Boulevard and in the front semicircular driveway of Dearborn Inn. (Courtesy of Walter P. Reuther Library, Wayne State University.)

Guests at Dearborn Inn could arrange with Independence Air Tours to take a flight from the Ford Airport. This c. 1931 photograph shows a Ford Tri-Motor with the image of the familiar watchman and his lantern pointing to the script, "The Dearborn Inn, Dearborn, Michigan." Flights were offered any day, except Sundays. (Courtesy of The Henry Ford, Acc. 1660, Box 121, 121-8, 56328.)

This June 1933 image shows the Dearborn Inn taxi shuttle parked at the curbside ready for service. The brickwork on the walkway is visible, as is the extensive detail of the window work, exterior light fixtures, and even the interior curtains. A July 3, 1931, article in the *Dearborn Independent* described, "The curtains or over-drapes bear similarity to the furniture used in the best colonial homes. There are three separate kinds of over-drapes and as many patterns of wall paper." (Courtesy of The Henry Ford, Acc. 1660, Box 121, 57700.)

This Treadway Inn's advertisement lists inns throughout Vermont, Massachusetts, Tennessee, Pennsylvania, New York, and Connecticut and describes the hotels as follows: "Notable for the Hospitable Welcome extended—an inheritance from Colonial days—for their good food, tastefully served, comfortable beds and moderate rates." The bottom of the ad lists two affiliated inns owned by Ford in Michigan and managed by L.G. Treadway Service Corporation of New York, which are the Botsford Tavern in Farmington and the Dearborn Inn in Dearborn. The original agreement between Oakwood Hotel Company and L.G. Treadway stated that the management firm would give the hotel "all reasonable advantages of advertising and publicity . . . and to display the name of the Inn" as part of the Treadway chain.

The portico shows amazing architectural details and appears to be a cool and relaxing place to sit. To keep guests comfortable in the summer, the Dearborn Inn would go on to be one of the first air-conditioned hotels in the world. The inn had 12 air-conditioned zones that could be individually regulated, and the cool temperatures made it popular with both tourists and locals who were trying to escape the heat of summer. John Packard, an early manager of the inn, stated that the hotel turned away more than 1,000 people during a summer heat wave in 1936 and that people were in the lobby waiting like hawks for someone to give up a room.

To this day, the hotel lobby possesses a very special charm. The portrait over the fireplace in this image remains in the inn's collection; however, a portrait of Henry Ford now hangs in this prestigious location. Behind the fireplace, the corridor connects the Early American Room (right) with the Old English Coffee Shop, known later as the Ten Eyck Tavern (left).

The *Dearborn Independent* reported the following on the opening of the hotel in July 1931: "The Inn has 108 guest rooms, each with private bath and shower, circulating ice water, full-length mirror, and radio. It also offers splendid dining room facilities, and has a modernly equipped coffee shop. Guests in the dining room are able to watch the flying field from their tables through the large dining room windows." The finest chefs served many dignitaries at the Early American Room, which was a regular dining venue for Henry and Clara Ford. (Courtesy of The Henry Ford, Acc. EI.67, Box 4, No. 83246-4.)

This postcard describes the main dining room as being "roomy—light and cheerful." The detail on the Chippendale chairs is clearly visible, and the tables are preset with dishes and silverware at each place setting. In the beginning, Ridgway and MacDonald & Gehm china with illustrations of historic Greenfield Village buildings graced the tables of the dining rooms, but by the 1950s similar Wedgwood china replaced the older china. Silver water pitchers, sugar and creamer sets, salt and pepper stands, and other items were crafted by International Silver and stamped "Dearborn Inn."

The Colonial Lounge is described as "a perfect setting for a game of bridge," but an early newspaper article described the hotel even more eloquently: "Early American in its architecture, the Dearborn Inn brings to this city a hostelry which harks back to the days when the country was in its infancy and the care of travelers was really a fine art. The atmosphere both inside and out is one likened to an old New England Inn. Interior decorations, furniture, and the general scheme are predominantly American."

The Old English Coffee Shop would later go on to become the space known as the Ten Eyck Tavern. This view clearly shows one of the two horseshoe-shaped counters that were installed when the hotel opened. Along the right edge of the photograph are opened doors leading down the hallway that connects the two dining areas. At the coffee shop, from a menu dated October 28, 1941, a visitor would have been able to enjoy one of many daily specials, including roast leg and rack of spring lamb with mint jelly for 90¢. It was served with a choice of fresh leaf spinach or mashed yellow turnips. (Courtesy of The Henry Ford, Acc. 1660, Box 121, 121-15, 56328-5e.)

The horseshoe-counter layout in the coffee shop must have proved inefficient or unpopular, because in this view both counters are gone and the room now accommodates guests at individual tables. The Old English Coffee Shop was a great place to enjoy "preserves, fruits, and cereals" for breakfast, or to stop in for "cold service, sandwiches, or salads" for lunch. A 1941 menu from the Dearborn Inn coffee shop reveals a cup of coffee was priced at a dime, but a cup of Sanka or Postum was 20¢. (Courtesy of The Henry Ford, Acc. EI.67, Box 4, #83246-5.)

The Italian marble floor from the main lobby reached around into this corridor and could be viewed around the edges of the carpet runner that connected the Old English Coffee Shop with the Early American Room. This image provides a closer look at the details of the floor coverings and wallpaper, as well as ceiling fixtures.

Each guest room was known to contain a scaled-down reproduction of an American drop-leaf pigeonhole desk, and a small blanket chest with a hammered wrought-iron design would be tucked in a corner or under a window in each room. As quoted in an interview for the *Detroit News*, the inn's assistant manager said, "Ninety percent of the people who check out of here want to know where they can buy one of those blanket chests." In this room, the chest is at the foot of the bed.

Each guest room was equipped with its own tub, shower/bath, full-length mirror, radio, and electric clock and was furnished with genuine old pieces from various parts of the country. This postcard notes, "Guest Rooms With Authentic Reproductions of Early American Pieces in Pine, Maple and Mahogany."

Here, the tree located in the center of the rear courtyard provides shade on a sunny summer afternoon. The car in the roadway is headed toward the garage entrance. In the distance is the Patrick Henry House, the largest of the cottages in the Colonial Village, which was built in 1937.

Until the Ford Airport closed, sightseeing trips in a Ford Tri-Motor plane were offered over Detroit and Windsor, Ontario. The quiet, countryside charm of the inn held much appeal for guests, who enjoyed activities such as tennis, badminton, horseback riding, and golf. In 1962, a 7,000-square-foot practice putting green was installed on the grounds of the hotel for guests and was lit for night use.

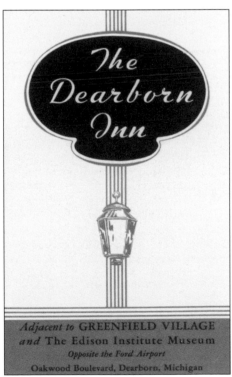

This is one of many brochures used to encourage guests to visit. With the headline "Every Comfort and Luxury," the brochure states, "Almost everything you could wish, you find already anticipated at the Dearborn Inn." Because Henry Ford was an avowed teetotaler and opponent of alcohol, rumors persist today that he would not allow the sale of alcoholic beverages at the inn. This brochure from the 1930s reports, "The finest wines and liquors are available." An original copy of the list of cocktails and wines is in the collection of the Benson Ford Research Center. A highball with rye—made with either Walker's Canadian Club or Seagram's VO—was 45¢ in a menu dated 1935.

The Dearborn Inn

THIS INN, TYPICAL OF EARLY AMERICAN HOSPITALITY AND ARCHITECTURE, EXPRESSES AN
IDEAL TRANSLATED INTO MODERN COMFORT AND CONVENIENCE

The Dearborn Inn stands in a delightful setting of thirteen acres of lawns, gardens and woods facing Oakwood Boulevard, with an open view of the Ford Airport and Greenfield Village. This Inn, recognized by experts as the finest construction of its kind in the world, is of a stately Georgian architecture that seems by its very design to present an aspect of gracious welcome to the traveler. ▲ ▲ ▲ Of almost surpassing charm is the spacious interior which is furnished in perfect reproductions of early American pieces in pine, maple, and mahogany. For the complete comfort of the guest, each of the one hundred and eight bedrooms is equipped with the most modern and luxurious appointments which include private bath and shower, circulating ice water, full length mirror, radio and electric clock. ▲ ▲ ▲ Removed from city and village, yet accessible to a metropolitan center, The Dearborn Inn is practically ideal in location. A sojourn of a day, a week or a month in its quiet and charming atmosphere can be crowded with interest and enjoyment. The Edison Institute of Technology offers Greenfield Village with its unique collection of historical buildings and Americana, as well as the many early handicrafts which are represented. Golf, on a fine eighteen hole course, and tennis are available, while stretches of open country invite the enthusiastic hiker. A magnificent view is to be had from the tiled roof promenade, where one may watch soaring airplanes and gorgeous sunsets. And when hunger calls, the guest may enjoy, either in the Early American Dining Room or the English Coffee Shop, the unexcelled cooking of a famous New England chef.

An early brochure describes the serene setting and many activities available at Dearborn Inn: "A sojourn of a day, a week or a month in its quiet and charming atmosphere can be crowded with interest and enjoyment. The Edison Institute of Technology offers Greenfield Village with its unique collection of historical buildings and Americana, as well as the many early handicrafts which are represented. Golf, on a fine eighteen-hole course, and tennis are available, while stretches of open country invite the enthusiastic hiker. A magnificent view is to be had from the tiled roof promenade, where one may watch soaring airplanes and gorgeous sunsets."

Welcome . . .

There is a design for living at the Dearborn Inn—an American Design. It is discovered in the stately Georgian architecture, in the various guest houses, the exterior of each a replica of some historical house in the country, in the broad lawns, the gardens and the woods. It is seen in the beautiful reproductions of early American furniture and decorations that grace the spacious interior. And it is felt in the application to the whole of the latest refinements and luxuries of modern invention.

With greatest care the Dearborn Inn was planned and built to one end—to welcome you with hospitality that is truly American.

The brochure continues, "With the greatest care the Dearborn Inn was planned and built to one end—to welcome you with hospitality that is truly American."

The Alexandria Ballroom was the first addition to expand the hotel in 1932. This photograph, which was taken in that room, is from the late 1930s and was found in the author's attic of her West Dearborn home. These individuals are dressed in various costumes and are believed to have been participants in one of the pageants celebrating Henry Ford's birthday. (Courtesy of Bertha Morris.)

Upon close examination of the large group photograph, the young man in the first row, second from the left, is wearing a bellman's cap. The emblem on the hat reads, "Dearborn Inn." (Courtesy of Bertha Morris.)

At this point in a trip, weary travelers might have wondered, "Are we there yet?" This billboard explains that the inn is just 11 miles down the road after turning left onto Allen Road. Allen turns into Pelham Road as it approaches Dearborn, and Pelham comes straight through to Oakwood Boulevard alongside the Dearborn Inn. This billboard mentions the inn being near the Ford Airport and the Early American Village, which would later be known as Greenfield Village. Currently, Greenfield Village is a part of The Henry Ford. (Courtesy of The Henry Ford, Acc. 833, Box 21, 57275-3.)

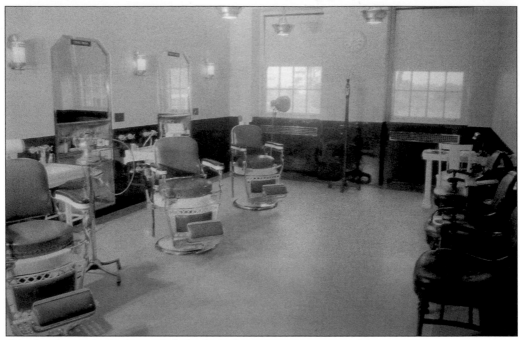

A barbershop, which also included a shoe-shine service, was one of the many guest conveniences at Dearborn Inn.

During World War II, the inn was known for having opened its doors to area teachers in an effort to relieve the local housing crunch. About this time, a room with a twin bed was $6 daily; a guest staying for 12 weeks or longer paid $14 a week, and a room was further discounted to $12.50 a week for teachers. (Courtesy of F. Serafino.)

Dearborn Inn remains an outstanding location for a wedding ceremony, reception, or honeymoon. This wedding party includes bridegroom Gerald G. Diehl and bride Marie Josephine Irving (fifth and sixth from the left), who were married at Holy Redeemer Catholic Church in southwest Detroit on April 19, 1947. Following the ceremony, the reception was held at Dearborn Inn, where the wedding party was photographed on the stairs facing the rear courtyard. (Courtesy of the Diehl family.)

The Detroit News

THE HOME NEWSPAPER FOR MORE THAN 70 YEARS

Largest Trading Area Circulation, Weekday and Sunday, of Any Michigan Newspaper

Night-Home Edition

Yanks Open Drive at Heart of Normandy

DEARBORN INN HELD UP

Reds Outflank 200,000 Germans in Minsk

Mask Pair Robs Clerk of $3,000	### War Bulletins		Cut Routes of Escape on 2 Sides	British Smash New Caen Blow
	Nazis Bar Civilians From Swiss Border	*Greeks Barred From Invasion Coasts*		
	Yanks Bomb Kuriles 2 Times in Week-End	*Curtin Seen Joint Control of Pacific Bases*		
	25 Rommel Tanks Wrecked in 24 Hours	*East Prussia Mobilizes as Reds Advance*		
	British Raiders Wreck Albanian Port	*Captive Nazi Gen. Reported Facing Trial*		Robots Blast at 2 Harbors
	Local Offers $890,000 for Henriot Killers			
	War Refugees Plead for Transfer to U.S.	*Yanks Wipe Out Suicide Force in Burma*		

The headline for the July 3, 1944, *Detroit News* reads, "Dearborn Inn Held Up." By July 7, the local *Dearborn Independent* newspaper reported, "Two confess to holding up Dearborn Inn." Night clerk Virginia Cleland was commended for sounding an air-raid alarm and for recognizing the "two masked bandits" as former bellboys at the inn, who approached the front desk at about 3:00 a.m. and escaped with $3,000. The article went on to state, "Detectives searched the grounds and found nearly a thousand dollars which the robbers had dropped in their haste to get away." (Courtesy of Dearborn Inn.)

Four

EXPANSION AND A COLONIAL VILLAGE

The doors opened to the hotel's first addition, the Alexandria Ballroom and Banquet Hall, on October 6, 1932. To celebrate, Henry and Clara Ford, along with their son, Edsel, and daughter-in-law, Eleanor, led 250 guests in a grand march to the ballroom for an evening of old-fashioned dancing, which was followed by a buffet supper.

In 1934, the Carrier Company installed air-conditioning in the hotel, and an expansion to the inn arrived just a few years later. Consideration was being given to adding guest rooms to the inn and creating separate housing for the staff, all in an effort to increase capacity and stave off operating losses. Ultimately, a collection of five guest cottages was built behind Dearborn Inn, and a dormitory was constructed alongside the hotel. The idea for cottages was based on a visit Edsel Ford made to California in 1935 to attend the San Diego International Exposition, where he saw guest cottages surrounding a main hotel building. He believed a similar arrangement would work at Dearborn Inn, and Charles Hart, an architect and vice president with the Treadway Service Corporation, was up for the task. It is Hart who is credited with the concept of the Colonial Village, which consists of replicas of historic homes that reflect an early American town around the inn. This village includes models of Edgar Allan Poe's cottage in Fordham, New York; Walt Whitman's farmhouse in Melville on Long Island, New York; Patrick Henry's mansion, "Red Hill," from Charlotte County, Virginia; Gov. Oliver Wolcott's house in Litchfield, Connecticut; and Barbara Fritchie's bungalow in Frederick, Maryland.

Although 18 cottages, a manager's house, and a swimming pool were originally planned, only five of the cottages were ready for guests by 1937, and unfortunately World War II curtailed plans for building the remaining houses and pool.

By the 1950s, a new US highway system increased the number of families traveling the nation by automobile. Thus, in 1958, talk was underway for another expansion. This time, two motor houses were planned to keep up with competition from local motels, and construction started in 1959. The Edison Institute has an entire collection of memos that were exchanged between Henry Ford Museum president Frank Caddy and executive director Donald Shelly regarding expansion plans. In addition, the museum has architectural drawings done by William Edward Kapp that show preliminary suggestions for converting the Dearborn Inn courtyard into a 227-person dining space.

Eventually, 54 guest rooms were added to the 132 rooms already available; these new rooms provided larger living spaces for families and convenient parking. The new addition featured rooms for families with two double beds and also suites for executives and bridal couples, which included a living room and at least one bedroom. All of these rooms and suites had private baths with usually a second lavatory in a dressing alcove.

Describing the new motor lodge, manager Richard McLain said that there was "a view of the inn's lawn from all rooms." The larger guesthouse was named the McGuffey Building, after pioneer American educator William Holmes McGuffey, and a second L-shaped building was named after botanist and naturalist Luther Burbank. Completely air-conditioned (as were the inn and cottages), the motor lodge was described as "modern as tomorrow" and was shown to the public at an open house on Sunday, August 28, 1960. Other modern touches included soft drinks, ice dispensers, magazines, newspapers, and sundries available in the office.

In May 1961, construction began on a heated 75-foot-by-42-foot swimming pool, an adjoining wading pool, and two diving boards, designed to provide relaxation and recreation for travelers. A swimming club was formed, giving residents access to the aquatic facilities.

An expansion to the dining facilities and kitchen also took place during this time span, and in 1961 the Dearborn Inn pioneered a new dial telephone system, eliminating some of the work for switchboard operators. Remodeling took place in the coffee shop about this same time, and it became known as the Ten Eyck Tavern. In 1965, the indoor parking garage was converted into the Greenfield Banquet Hall, allowing for additional dining space for large private parties; the space was referred to as the nation's first hotel with a drive-in exhibit hall.

This was not the last addition, or even the largest, that Dearborn Inn would undergo. Word hit the streets during the summer of 1987 that Dearborn Inn would close for renovations in November. A headline in the *Detroit News* stated, "Renovations to Shut Hotel for Six Months," but ultimately the inn was closed for 18 months. At an estimated cost of $25 million, plans included expansion of 66 additional guest rooms; a new ballroom to accommodate 650 people; relocation of three cottages; complete renovation of existing guest rooms and new interior decor; an entirely new pool, tennis courts, a health center, and weight room; and new exterior lighting and landscaping. In April 1989, the Dearborn Inn reopened its doors having been restored, renovated, and refurbished.

It was an amazing transformation that modernized Henry Ford's "modern" hotel while keeping the same feel it had when the doors first opened in 1931.

Just slightly more than a year after the doors of Dearborn Inn opened in the summer of 1931, a significant construction project was underway to add the Alexandria Ballroom over the garage. (Courtesy of Bentley Historical Library, University of Michigan, Albert Kahn Dearborn Inn, Box 10, Folder 1504.)

Here, the doors to the garage are being propped open, and vehicles are lined up in the parking lot. Various chutes have been set up to lower construction debris to the ground safely. (Courtesy of Bentley Historical Library, University of Michigan.)

Once the skeleton of the roof was raised, it provided the distinctive shape to both the exterior of the building and the interior of the room. The details inside the Alexandria Ballroom are modeled after a ballroom Henry Ford admired in Alexandria, Virginia, believed to be the ballroom in the historic Gadsby's Tavern. The architecture in that original ballroom was so well noted that elements have been removed and displayed at the Metropolitan Museum of Art in New York City. The curved ceiling in Dearborn Inn's Alexandria Ballroom was designed to improve acoustics, similar to the ceiling Henry Ford had installed when remodeling and expanding the ballroom at the Botsford Inn. (Courtesy of Bentley Historical Library, University of Michigan.)

The courtyard is off to the right edge in this photograph. The walls surrounding the new ballroom are up, and work is taking place on the roof. There is barely a visible difference in the matching of the bricks. A new doorway has been cut into the first floor leading outdoors, just to the right of the garage doors. (Courtesy of Bentley Historical Library, University of Michigan.)

Though construction materials remain alongside the base of the garage, the roof and much of the exterior work are nearing completion in this photograph. (Courtesy of Bentley Historical Library, University of Michigan.)

Dancing was important to Henry and Clara Ford, and they provided dance lessons to Ford employees and area school students. They also hosted dances in their home, at Botsford Inn, on the dance floor at the Ford Engineering Building, and later in the ballroom at Lovett Hall, which was constructed at Greenfield Village. Since 1932, the Alexandria Ballroom has been hosting parties, events, and celebrations, including formal dances such as this. (Courtesy of The Henry Ford, Acc. 1660, Box 121, 121-15, 7710.)

A May 1932 memo from the auditing department indicates that 17 employees were living at the inn at that time. The building shown here is the Helps' Dormitory, which was constructed alongside the inn in 1936 to free up the use of hotel rooms for paying guests. With the L.G. Treadway Company managing "Real New England Inns" throughout the East Coast, many staff members were brought to Dearborn from the East to work at the inn. This structure still stands, but it is used for storage; a carpenter's shop exists in the basement.

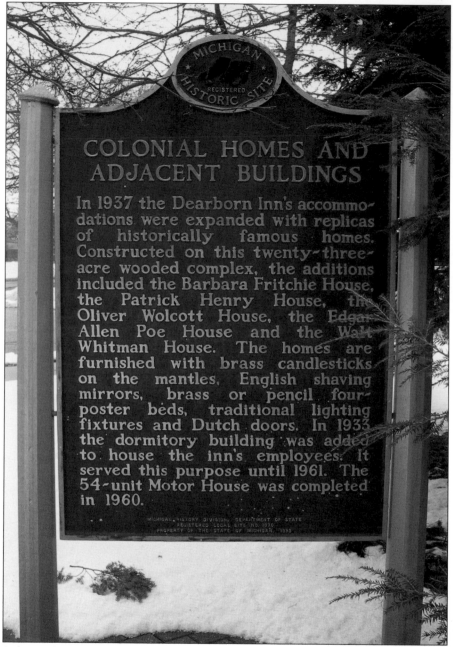

COLONIAL HOMES AND ADJACENT BUILDINGS

In 1937 the Dearborn Inn's accommodations were expanded with replicas of historically famous homes. Constructed on this twenty-three-acre wooded complex, the additions included the Barbara Fritchie House, the Patrick Henry House, the Oliver Wolcott House, the Edgar Allen Poe House and the Walt Whitman House. The homes are furnished with brass candlesticks on the mantles, English shaving mirrors, brass or pencil four-poster beds, traditional lighting fixtures and Dutch doors. In 1933 the dormitory building was added to house the inn's employees. It served this purpose until 1961. The 54-unit Motor House was completed in 1960.

MICHIGAN HISTORY DIVISION, DEPARTMENT OF STATE
REGISTERED LOCAL SITE NO. 1070
PROPERTY OF THE STATE OF MICHIGAN, 1995

This Michigan State Historic Site Marker provides the following information about the Colonial Village and adjacent buildings: "In 1937 the Dearborn Inn's accommodations were expanded with replicas of historically famous homes. Constructed on this 23-acre wooded complex, the additions included the Barbara Fritchie House, the Oliver Wolcott House, the Edgar Allen Poe House and the Walt Whitman House. The homes are furnished with brass candlesticks on the mantles, English shaving mirrors, brass or pencil four-poster beds, traditional lighting fixtures and Dutch doors. In 1933 the dormitory building was added to house the inn's employees. It served this purpose until 1961. The 54-unit Motor House was completed in 1960." Note that the dormitory was actually constructed during the summer of 1936.

The Barbara Fritchie House is entered by way of a rose arbor for each door. When constructed, there was a wrought-iron foot scraper on the doorstep to the bungalow and a plain doorknocker on only one of the two front doors. An American flag is flown out of the second-floor dormer window where the 95-year-old Fritchie, immortalized in the John Greenleaf Whittier poem, waved her Union flag at passing Confederate troops. "Shoot if you must, this old gray head / But spare your country's flag," states the poem named after Fritchie.

The Barbara Fritchie House in Frederick, Maryland (pictured), and the replica at Dearborn Inn have numerous interior and exterior differences. A 1940s magazine article about the cottages suggests that Maryland and Michigan could have another "War between the States" contending for the more authentic replica. The original Barbara Fritchie House was partially destroyed by a flood in 1868. Dearborn Inn's Fritchie House was constructed from original plans and other reference information. (Photograph by Andrew Ganem.)

A 1937 magazine *Hotel Monthly* describes the quality construction of the five Colonial Village cottages: "Foundations, flooring, supports, walls, plaster, ceilings, bathroom fixtures—all are the finest. Incidentally, both walls and ceiling are metal lath and plaster." (Courtesy of Henry Ford Centennial Library.)

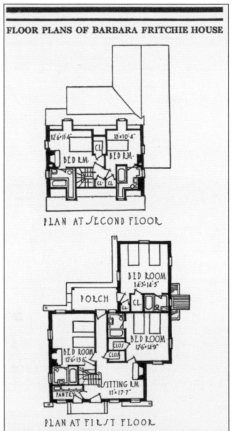

FLOOR PLANS OF BARBARA FRITCHIE HOUSE

PLAN AT SECOND FLOOR

PLAN AT FIRST FLOOR

The interior of the Barbara Fritchie replica was reconfigured to provide the greatest number of guest rooms, and a bathroom was created, instead of a hallway, with the dormer window out of which Fritchie waved her flag. (Courtesy of Henry Ford Centennial Library.)

This interior image of a bedroom in the Barbara Fritchie House shows two full-size beds, a night stand with a lamp, a blanket chest, desk and chair, desk blotter, floor lamp, arm chair, floor rug, and a single candlestick on the window ledge. The wallpaper, curtains, window shades, and bedspreads add a warm, welcoming feel to this comfortable room. One of these two beds is currently owned by the author and includes a footboard plaque explaining it is a replica from the Barbara Fritchie House. This photograph is from 1937, when the Colonial Village cottages were first opened. (Courtesy of The Henry Ford, Acc. 1660, Box 121, 188-21082.)

This small brass plaque is affixed to the footboard of a bed from the Barbara Fritchie House. Furnishings from Dearborn Inn and the Colonial Village cottages were sold during a huge renovation that took place from 1987 to 1989. (Courtesy of Paul F. Ganem.)

Spring cleaning at the inn was reported in the *Dearborn Press & Guide* newspaper in April 1977. Each of the five cottages behind the inn received "fresh coats of paint inside and new wallpaper and carpeting where needed." Seen here is the Oliver Wolcott House. The entrance is of pure Colonial design, with fluted columns supporting the corniced roof, and over the doorway is a half-moon transom window.

The original home of Governor Wolcott, shown here in Litchfield, Connecticut, did not initially have a porch, but one was added in 1800. By including this wing on the replica, a porch and an extra bedroom were included. The screened-in porch provides a place for guests to relax.

One exterior feature on the Oliver Wolcott House was the black band around the white brick chimney, a mark of identification used during the Revolution to show the occupant's political affiliations. (Courtesy of Henry Ford Centennial Library.)

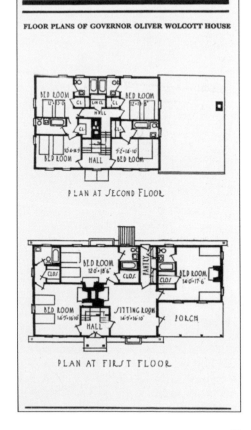

FLOOR PLANS OF GOVERNOR OLIVER WOLCOTT HOUSE

PLAN AT SECOND FLOOR

PLAN AT FIRST FLOOR

Guests to Gov. Oliver Wolcott's original house included Alexander Hamilton and General Lafayette, and General Washington was a known visitor as well. (Courtesy of Henry Ford Centennial Library.)

When Patrick Henry retired from his political career, he purchased Red Hill Plantation in 1794. The original structure was a small dwelling, and he later added a little shed because he wanted to hear rain on the roof. Of the five cottages in the Colonial Village, this is one of two houses where old records were used for reconstruction since the original Red Hill was destroyed by fire in 1920.

Red Hill was furnished with canopied beds and afforded visitors an opportunity to experience sleeping in an exact replica of such an antique. The canopies were covered in sheer material, with ball fringe for the edging to match the candlewick bedspreads. While the rugs were hooked by machine, the designs were of handcrafted styles. (Courtesy of Henry Ford Centennial Library.)

FLOOR PLANS OF PATRICK HENRY HOUSE

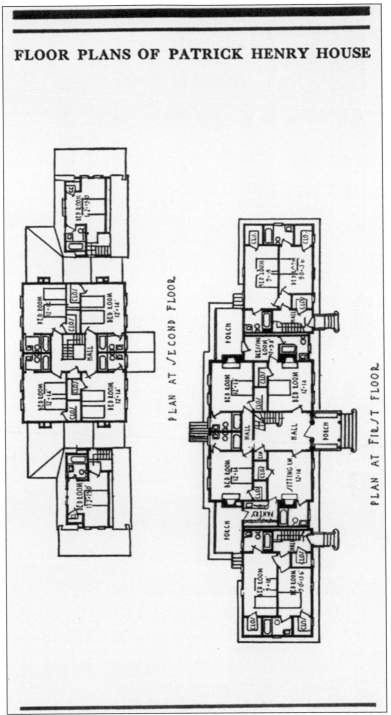

The Patrick Henry House is the largest of the five cottages in the Colonial Village. With two wings, it has a sitting room and 13 bedrooms, each with a bath and closet. The layouts for the two wings of the house were identical with two bedrooms on the first floor and one on the second floor. (Courtesy of Henry Ford Centennial Library.)

An article in the May 1940 magazine *American Home* describes details of the Colonial Village. It states, "The trimmings to the windows and doors on the inside are replicas of those in the real homes, as are the hearths and mantels of slate and marble. The doors and hardware are likewise copies of originals. Old sconces and candelabra, which were either in the first house or of a period when it was in its glory, were copied in making the electric fixtures for all the rooms. Likewise, the furniture, wherever possible, is an exact reproduction of that used by the famous owners in their day."

"The Poe Cottage, the smallest of the buildings having just two rooms, is sometimes rented for long periods of time," stated a 1976 *Dearborn Times-Herald* newspaper article. "An executive who has a home in another state, but spends much time in Dearborn, has rented a room in one of the houses for five years."

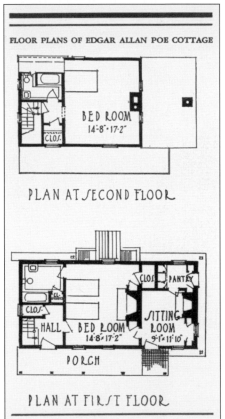

FLOOR PLANS OF EDGAR ALLAN POE COTTAGE

BED ROOM
14'-8" · 17'-2"
CLOS.

PLAN AT SECOND FLOOR

CLOS. PANTRY
CLOS.
HALL BED ROOM SITTING ROOM
14'-8"·17'-2" 9'-1"·11'-10"
PORCH

PLAN AT FIRST FLOOR

The modest clapboard Edgar Allan Poe Cottage was constructed with a brass doorknocker representing a lion's head. The cottage was replicated from the original in Fordham, New York, where Poe lived for three years with his wife, Virginia, and her mother. It is believed it was there that the great poet wrote "The Bells," "Ulalume," "Annabel Lee" and *Eureka.* (Courtesy of Henry Ford Centennial Library.)

When furnishing the Edgar Allan Poe Cottage and the other houses, authentic and period pieces of original furniture were sought and then reproduced. The woodwork in the Colonial Village houses was painted white after the style of the times or left with plain knotty pine finish where appropriate. (Courtesy of Henry Ford Centennial Library.)

Author Arthur Hailey wrote the following note in the Dearborn Inn guest registry documenting his stay in the Poe Cottage: "During a large part of 1968 and early 1969, the Poe Cottage of The Dearborn Inn was my working headquarters while researching a new novel (tentative title: *WHEELS*) about the auto industry, to follow *AIRPORT, HOTEL, THE FINAL DIAGNOSIS,* etc. I am exceedingly grateful to Dick McLain and his efficient staff for making my stay pleasant and memorable, and somehow I shall work The Dearborn Inn into my story . . . Arthur Hailey." (Courtesy of Dearborn Inn.)

Mounted over the front door of the Poe Cottage, this raven is sheltered by the porch roof.

87

Walt Whitman was born in 1819 in the original of this replicated structure, which was located in West Hills, New York. In building the Colonial Village structures, ceiling heights had to be adjusted to accommodate for pipes, wires, and ductwork. Wherever it could be done, building materials exactly like the original were used on the exteriors; on the Walt Whitman House, this included cedar shingles.

The bedrooms in the Walt Whitman House included a chintz-covered chair and pine chair with a seat woven of splints. The beds were described as simple, with candlewick bedspreads and tall wooden candlestick holders placed on the mantel. (Courtesy of Henry Ford Centennial Library.)

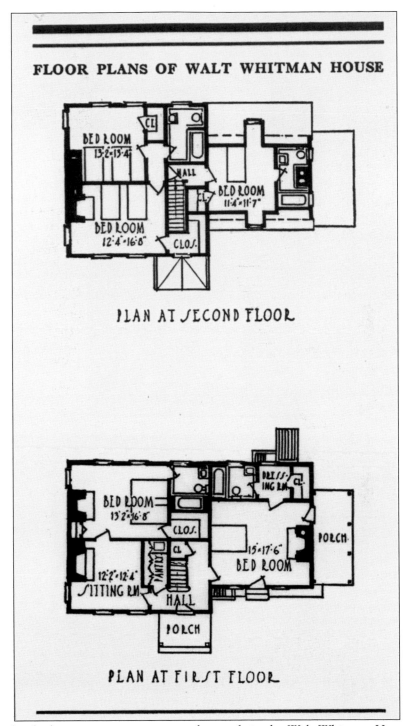

FLOOR PLANS OF WALT WHITMAN HOUSE

PLAN AT SECOND FLOOR

PLAN AT FIRST FLOOR

There are five bedrooms, a sitting room, and a porch in the Walt Whitman House. Some of the bedrooms are single and some double, but the furnishings in all of them were originally similar. White voile curtains with ruffles hung from the windows. (Courtesy of Henry Ford Centennial Library.)

Various plans were considered for constructing an office to conveniently accommodate guests arriving for a stay in one of the two detached motor house facilities. One proposal called for a drive-up window where motorists could check in without leaving their vehicle.

The McGuffey Motor House, seen here, was named after the author of the famous McGuffey Reader textbooks. The second motor-house facility was named after botanist Luther Burbank.

This marketing brochure for Dearborn Inn features a nighttime image of the hotel with dramatic lighting that draws attention to the beautiful architecture of the arches in the portico. (Courtesy of Adrian A. de Vogel.)

The new motor-house facilities featured spacious room accommodations ideal for families, as well as suites suitable for newlyweds.

Delicious food... choice of atmospheres

Maine lobsters . . . prime steaks . . . steamed clams . . . roasts simmering in their own juices . . . fishes from the cold Atlantic . . . Is it any wonder Dearborn Inn is well known for its robust meals? Enjoy, enjoy . . . in the intimate atmosphere of the Ten Eyck Tavern . . . the Early American room . . . or Golden Eagle Lounge . . . where every weekday you'll find featured a business buffet. Dinners and banquets for up to 350 are served in the Alexandria Ballroom . . . patterned after a similar room discovered by Henry Ford I in Alexandria, Virginia.

Delightful Seafood Fantasy . . . among the specialties of the house are garden fresh salads, steaks, chops and seafoods topped off with mouth-watering desserts.

There's always something to do at the Dearborn Inn

An AAU-sized, heated swimming pool with two diving boards and spacious decks . . . a wading area and a playground for tots . . . regulation-size tennis courts . . . shuffleboard courts . . . and within minutes, a public golf course . . . for fun around the clock. Just across the street is world famous Greenfield Village and Henry Ford Museum . . . among the top ten tourist attractions in the country!

This brochure promoting Dearborn Inn declares, "There's always something to do," and that guests can expect "delicious food." Photographs show the outdoor pool and motor house, the tennis courts, fine dining in the Early American Room, and casual dining in the Ten Eyck Tavern. (Courtesy of Adrian A. deVogel.)

This interior photograph of a guest room provides a glimpse of how early-American furnishings were blended together with modern details, such as a television. Note the blanket chest pictured in the lower left corner. (Courtesy of Adrian A. deVogel.)

The blanket chest glimpsed in the lower left corner of the photograph at the top of the page can be seen here in full view. These beautifully crafted chests came in several styles and were fixtures in guest rooms. (From the family collection of chef Paul LeVeque.)

In the above view of the hotel's lobby, flames can be seen in the fireplace, and a sign labeled "Dining Room" is visible in the open doorway leading to the Early American Room. The original chandeliers, seen below, still hang in the lobby, and today a portrait of Henry Ford hangs over the mantle. A tradition for many Ford Motor Company retirees is to have a luncheon at the inn and have a photograph taken alongside Ford's portrait. (Courtesy of Adrian A. deVogel.)

Five

A PIECE OF HISTORY

While Dearborn Inn continues to possess the similar charm that visitors experienced in the 1930s, it is interesting to note how it has been perceived throughout the years. A booklet printed in 1951 describes a visit to the inn in great detail. Published by Richard Bennett Talcott, *The Letter Booklet* was a multipage pamphlet that could be mailed, similar to a postcard. In part, the following describes a visit to Dearborn Inn:

> When I drove up to the door I felt for a minute that I was visiting a southern colonial Inn, for its stately Georgian architecture belies its modernity. Beautifully landscaped lawns and gardens further enhance its seeming antiquity.
>
> There was no question about the genuineness of the hospitality for I was warmly welcomed by my hosts who took a keen personal interest in making my stay as pleasant as possible. This friendliness, overlooked at many hostelries in today's press of business, proved very refreshing and enabled me to learn interesting things about the Inn that I might otherwise have never known.
>
> My bellboy, for example, told me as he put my luggage in the bedroom, that Dearborn Inn was the first completely air conditioned hotel in the country. Of course, I raised my window out of habit although he had assured me that it was quite unnecessary. It seems they keep all the rooms at an even and comfortable temperature throughout the year.
>
> And while I'm on the subject of bedrooms, I'd just like to say that my room here is one of the most comfortable that I've ever been in. It's attractively furnished with reproductions of colonial pieces which, I understand, were manufactured especially for the Inn. The wallpaper is tastefully decorated with colonial scenes, and my bedside table houses a radio. It's a homey room that surely must have been planned for real relaxation.
>
> I went around to the front of the Inn and crossed a broad highway to walk past the Ford Airport and in less than ten minutes was at the Museum where there began one of the most interesting experiences I've ever had. I got back to the Inn with a ravenous appetite, and after dressing headed for the Early American dining room where I was served one of the most delicious meals I have ever eaten.
>
> Not that I want to make your mouth water—but I had bluepoints on the half shell to start things off in the proper manner. I could have had some of their onion soup which I was told by another of the guests is out of this world.

You'll also enjoy eating out of the Wedgwood china which was manufactured especially for the Inn. The hand painted ware shows scenes in Greenfield Village and is really very effective.

Incidentally, I ate several of my meals in the English coffee shop where dining is more informal and very pleasant. This is a very attractive room where paneling runs three quarters of the way from the floor to the ceiling.

After dinner I relaxed in one of the deep, comfortable chairs that are scattered conveniently about the spacious lobby and listened to an organ recital that included a lot of light classical music. You know, the kind you love to hear—music that makes you feel good all over like selections from the Red Mill. They have a concert like it most every night and on Sunday afternoons.

When the concert was over I repaired to the Colonial Cocktail Lounge which is one of the most attractive I have seen anywhere. The atmosphere is congenial—and I'll wager that the bartender makes the best drinks in the whole state of Michigan.

While I was there I got to talking with some of the other guests who told me a number of interesting things about the Inn. It was originally built, I learned, to provide accommodations for fliers who landed at the Ford Airport which is just across the street. Back in the middle twenties there was quite a lot of activity there and a number of air meets took place annually. It was at such time that the Inn was filled to capacity.

One of the guests told me that there's a special group of rooms known as "Pilot's Row." This name was given it in the old days when the section was occupied chiefly by pilots.

Although the average visitor to Dearborn Inn spends most of his time at Greenfield Village and the Museum, there are many other interesting things to do. I discovered that it wasn't necessary to leave the Inn to fill any of my normal needs. Why, there's even a barber shop here. As for other diversion—well, there's a fine game room where I spent a few hours playing pool and table tennis.

There was only one thing wrong with my visit. I wasn't able to stay as long as I would have liked.

As the years rolled by, there would be plenty of reasons why other guests to Dearborn Inn would wish they could extend their stay, too, and to possess special memories and keepsakes that would become part of history.

This "Letter Booklet" provided a first-person description of visiting Dearborn Inn and includes great detail about the food: "Although I chose steak, I could have had lobster which I understand comes in here fresh every day from New England. Lake Michigan trout was on the menu, too, along with Jumbo Whitefish. Many other intriguing entrees were offered, among them frogs legs for which the inn is famous. The wide choice of desserts would delight any gourmet's heart, but when you come here take my advice and try the Dutch apple pie. You'll love it."

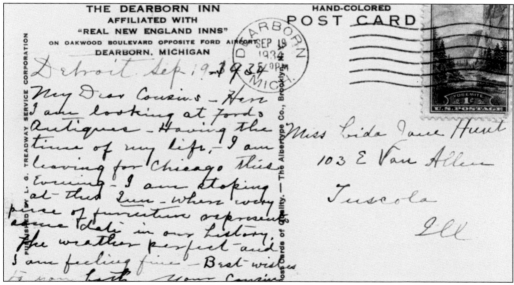

This Dearborn Inn postcard was mailed from Detroit on September 19, 1934. The sender writes, "My Dear Cousins—Here I am looking at Ford's antiques. Having the time of my life. I am leaving for Chicago this evening. I am stoping [sic] at this Inn where every piece of furniture represents some date in our history. The weather's perfect and I am feeling fine. Best wishes to you both. Your cousin." Today, visitors can still "look at Ford's antiques" and stop at this amazing Inn; however, there are no guarantees on the weather.

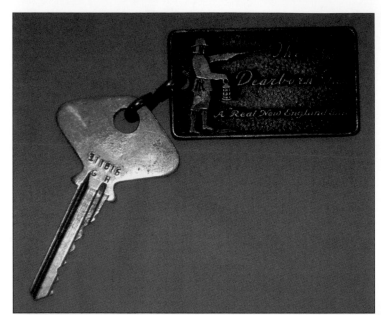

Here is an early key and heavy fob, bearing the mark of the watchman and the phrase "A 'Real New England Inn,'" to the door of Dearborn Inn guest room 86.

A skeleton-shaped key fit the door to room 53. Keys for the houses in the Colonial Village were carried on round brass fobs, such as these, marked "PH" for the Patrick Henry House, "WW" for the Walt Whitman House, and so on. Postage was paid by the Dearborn Inn for returning a room key by mail.

Small bars of Lux brand soap wrapped in a paper label from Dearborn Inn were used in the guest rooms for the main hotel, as well as the Colonial Village and motor lodges. Guests who sent garments to be laundered by the hotel staff were informed, on the inn's laundry receipt, "Special attention will be given your silks and woolens. We wash them by hand in lukewarm water with Lux."

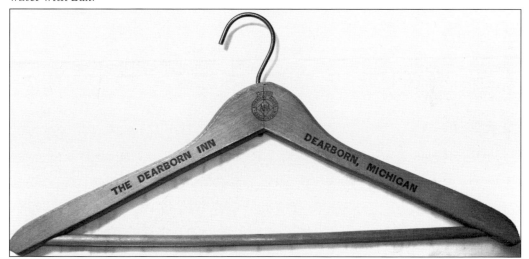

As indicated by the stamp on this hanger, the Dearborn Inn was a member of the American Hotel Association. In a 1958 *Dearborn Guide* newspaper interview, inn manager Richard McLean stated, "Perhaps one of the most irritating annoyances with which a hotel manager has to contend is the disappearance of such items as silver, linens, and towels by souvenir hunters [to put it kindly]. Certainly, I have found the problem a provoking one at times, particularly when—as in one case—a complete set of linens, towels, and bath mat disappeared. But, actually, here at the inn that problem is such a comparatively small one—infinitesimal considering our volume of business—that I try to overlook it and never let it destroy my faith in the goodness of people."

When guests entered the main Early American Room, they saw charger plates and place settings already arranged on the tables, which were covered in white linens. Plates similar to the one shown were made by both Ridgway and MacDonald & Gehm and were used well into the 1950s. The plates included illustrations of historic buildings, including Dearborn Inn (pictured) and at least a dozen other images, mostly structures on display in Greenfield Village. When these original plates were retired, Wedgwood made similar plates for use at the inn with illustrations of many of the same buildings.

Silver pitchers were used in the Early American Room and can be seen in photographs from the 1930s and 1940s. Many items were made by International Silver, with "Dearborn Inn" engraved on the underside. Henry and Clara Ford dined at Dearborn Inn regularly and had a favorite table in the main dining room, which was located where Henry Ford could view who was coming and going from the front door of the inn, as well as who was arriving at the entrance of the dining room.

Dearborn Inn was always a special place for children to visit, too. With a playground, and later a swimming pool, the inn extended hospitality to families in many different ways. In the dining room, children were provided special china, including plates, mugs, and bowls, with images of popular nursery rhymes. (From the family collection of chef Paul LeVeque.)

Meals in the main dining room were not the only option for guests, particularly for late arrivals and early risers. This 1941 menu from the Old English Coffee Shop featured daily specials of cocktails and soups; entrees and roasts, which included vegetables and potatoes; and desserts. The coffee shop later became the Ten Eyck Tavern, named after Conrad Ten Eyck, who opened lodging in Dearborn in 1826 on Michigan Avenue, then known as the Chicago Road.

A LA CARTE MENU
COFFEE SHOP

COCKTAILS AND SOUPS

Tomato Juice .20	Orange Juice .20	Cranberry Juice .20
Fresh Fruit Cocktail .40		Oyster Cocktail .50
	Fresh Shrimp Cocktail .45	
Consomme, per cup .20		Chicken Bouillon .20
Cream of Tomato .25		Soup du Jour .20
	Oyster Cream Stew .75	

RELISHES

Iced Celery .20	Queen or Stuffed Olives .25	Celery and Olives .25
Spiced Watermelon .20		Spiced Peaches .20
Piccalilli .20	Chow Chow .20	Sweet Mixed Pickles .20

STEAKS AND CHOPS (Cooked to Order)

Sirloin $1.75	Tenderloin $1.50
Sirloin a la Minute $1.50	Lamb Chops (2) $1.25, Single .75
Veal or Pork Chops (2) $1.00, Single .60	
Broiled Bacon (6 slices) .60	Ham Steak $1.00
Boston Baked Beans .35	
Potato, Vegetable (from regular menu), Rolls and Butter Served with all Meat Orders	

EGGS

Boiled, Fried, Scrambled, Poached, Shirred .35	
Plain Omelette .40	Cheese or Jelly Omelette .50
Bacon or Ham and Eggs .75	
Rolls or Toast served with all Egg Orders	

COLD SERVICE

Assorted Cold Cuts with Chicken $1.00	
Ham .90	Roast Beef $1.00
Chicken $1.10	Turkey $1.10	Sardines .75
Liverwurst or Bologna .80	
Potato Salad and Rolls served with Cold Meat Orders	

SALADS

Hearts of Lettuce .40	Waldorf .60	Chicken $1.00
Vegetable Combination .50		Fruit Supreme .80
Crab Meat $1.00	Potato .40	Tuna Fish .75
Tomato and Cucumber .55		Pineapple, Cheese and Nut .60
Dressings: French, Russian, Mayonnaise.		
Rolls and Butter served with all Salad Orders		

SANDWICHES

Ham .30	Egg .25	Tomato, Lettuce and Mayonnaise .30
American Cheese .25	Sliced Chicken .60	Ham and Egg .50
Club .80	Ham and Cheese .45	Peanut Butter .25
Cream Cheese and Olive .30		Cream Cheese and Jelly .30
Chicken Salad .50	Sardine .45	Egg Salad .40
Hamburger .35		Roast Beef .60

PASTRY AND ICE CREAM

Pie .15	a la Mode .25	Pudding .15
	Assorted Cake and Macaroons .25	
Sherbet .15	Ice Cream .20	Sundaes .25

PRESERVES, FRUITS AND CEREALS

Orange Marmalade .20	Raspberry Jam .20	Strawberry Jam .20
	Currant Jelly .20	
Sliced Orange .20	Stewed Prunes .20	Figs in Syrup .20
Half Grapefruit .20	Sliced Bananas .20	Preserved Figs .20
	All Cereals with Cream .30	
Shredded Wheat	Bran Flakes	Wheaties
Puffed Rice	Puffed Wheat	All Bran	Grape Nuts
Corn Flakes	Oatmeal	Cream of Wheat	Wheatena

CHEESE (Served with Crackers)

American .25	Swiss .25	Old English .30	Gruyere .40
Cottage .25	Cream .30	Roquefort .45	Cheddar .35

DRINKS

	Coffee, per pot .15	Cup .10
Tea, per pot .15	Iced Tea .15	Iced Coffee .15
Sanka .20	Postum .20	Cocoa, pot pot .15
Milk .10	Buttermilk .10	Malted Milk .25

TOAST AND GRIDDLE CAKES

Dry .10	Buttered .10	Cinnamon .25
Milk .30	Cream .40	Melba .15
	French Toast with Syrup or Jelly .60	
Griddle Cakes with Vermont Maple Syrup .40		With Bacon .50
	Waffle with Syrup or Honey .45	
Muffins .10		Rolls .10
Crackers and Milk .25		With Cream .35

SODA BAR

Ice Cream .20	Sherbet .15	Sundaes .25
Sodas (with Ice Cream) .25		Milk Shakes .25
Malted Milk Shakes .25		Coca Cola .15
Boston Cooler (Ginger Ale and Ice Cream) .30		
Fresh Fruit Orangeade or Lemonade .30		
Flavors (Chocolate, Pineapple, Vanilla and Strawberry)		
Canada Dry Ginger Ale (Splits) .20		Pints .35

The Old English Coffee Shop menu allowed for à la carte orders, which were popular lunch items with local businessmen. This menu lists "Steaks and Chops (cooked to order)" and also an oyster cocktail for 50¢, spiced watermelon for 20¢, a sardine sandwich for 45¢, and a selection of cheeses served with crackers.

Dearborn Inn has always been a popular destination for newlyweds to host wedding receptions. This English-made, stainless-steel knife with a hand-painted, ceramic handle was a gift and keepsake from the inn to happy couples for cutting their wedding cakes. (From the family collection of chef Paul LeVeque.)

Dearborn Inn's lore indicates that smoking was not permitted at the hotel until after Henry Ford's death in 1947; however, photographs dating before this clearly show ashtrays throughout the inn. One photograph taken of the Fords at a Dearborn Inn banquet reveals a matchbook and ashtray set right in front of Henry Ford. This image of a wooden cigar box likely dates to the 1940s. It is possible that the "no tobacco" rule may have just pertained to cigarettes at Dearborn Inn; cigars may have been the exception.

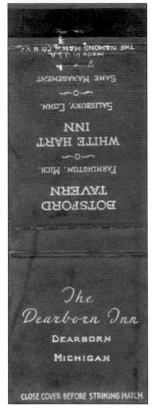

The design on the cover of this matchbook for Dearborn Inn was also used at the Botsford Tavern and at White Hart Inn and states, "Same Management."

The "First Day of Issue" of the 12¢ Henry Ford stamp took place at Greenfield Village in 1968 and coincided with Ford's birthday on July 30. The Dearborn Stamp Club issued this cover, which includes an interior card declaring Dearborn Inn as "The World's First 'Airport Hotel,'" which is still a common belief of many.

In 1926, the first US Airmail flight took place between Dearborn, Michigan, and Cleveland, Ohio. In 1958, the flight was reenacted, and this commemorative cover was released.

Six

TRANSITIONS AND
TRADITIONAL EXCELLENCE

When the 50th anniversary of Dearborn Inn rolled around in July 1981, a four-day birthday celebration took place at the inn. Manager Adrian deVogel and chef George Riley proudly displayed a five-tiered cake featuring the signature Dearborn Inn lantern logo in a photograph that appeared in the *Dearborn Press & Guide*. Two years later, a June 2, 1983, article in the *Dearborn Times-Herald* stated, "The Dearborn Inn was hailed as a symbol of pride and character at the unveiling of a plaque marking the designation of the 52-year-old landmark as a Michigan State Historic Site, May 23. Its designation as a national historic place was announced concurrently."

Dearborn Inn had been open more than 50 years, was consistently receiving awards and high marks for outstanding service from prestigious organizations such as the Mobil Travel Guide and AAA, and was now recognized as both a state and national historic site. However, the horizon was uncertain for the future of the inn.

As a wholly owned subsidiary of the Edison Institute, the inn was given to the organization in 1953 to provide added operating revenue for the Henry Ford Museum and Greenfield Village. By 1982, rumors were flying and headlines in the local papers seemed to have the inside scoop—Dearborn Inn was going to be sold.

Plans for a major expansion of the inn had already been drawn up the previous year; however, the incoming president of the Edison Institute questioned whether the inn was central to the mission of the organization. Representatives from the Edison Institute and the hotel denied rumors of the inn being for sale, but 10 months after the story had been reported in the *Dearborn Press & Guide*, an editorial by Gary Woronchak stated, "The fact remains that the Dearborn Inn—as we said—will be sold."

Eventually, an investment group was identified as the soon-to-be owner of the inn, but the transaction ultimately did not materialize. Then, an announcement in the *Detroit Free Press* came from Ford Motor Company chairman Phillip Caldwell on January 17, 1984, which stated that Ford "will buy the Dearborn Inn for an undisclosed sum from the Edison Institute." The *Detroit News* quoted Caldwell as saying, "We will want to do some refurbishing and improvement and that sort of thing. But we want it to be a place where people appreciate the heritage of the past and can feel the warmth and hospitality of the kind of company we'd like to be."

Just three years later, in 1987, the Lincoln Hotel Corporation, the management company of Dearborn Inn, made a joint announcement with Ford Motor Land Development Corporation chairman Wayne Doran. In the statement, both parties agreed to a major expansion and renovation, which would close the doors of the inn for 18 months, but that time would help preserve it for generations. When completed, 66 additional rooms were constructed, new banquet facilities were added, the historic cottages were refurbished with three of them relocated, the interior décor was updated throughout, a health center was added, and landscaping and improvements took place outdoors.

Under the operation of Marriott International, 50 guests with reservations began arriving at 7:00 a.m. on the day Dearborn Inn reopened in April 1989. John F. Nehman wrote the following in the April 25 edition of the *Detroit News*:

> In the lobby—which retains the original checkerboard marble floor, cracks and all—the original furniture, restored and replaced, includes two sets of partner desks, Chippendale piecrust tables, sheaf-back chairs and a large Chippendale curio cabinet with a radio in the bottom. A portrait of Henry Ford, painted by artist John S. Coppin a year after Ford's death in 1947, hangs over a green marble fireplace.

All was well. The Dearborn Inn was reopened for business, and the history of the magnificent hotel was marching onward.

When it opened, the L.G. Treadway Service Corporation provided management services for Dearborn Inn and used its own slogan, "A Real New England Inn," on marketing materials. The familiar silhouette of a watchman pointing the way and holding a lantern was a Treadway logo used on signage, letterhead, and other printed materials.

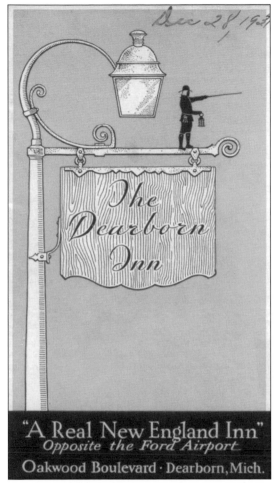

When Seaboard Properties took over the inn in 1939, Treadway Service markings were discontinued and an illustration of a horse-drawn carriage began to appear as a replacement. By the time the motor lodge opened in 1960, an image of a distinctive lamppost, surrounded by the warm glow of light, was being used as the inn's corporate logo. The rights to the Treadway name currently belong to the last remaining hotel in the Treadway chain, the Owego Treadway Inn and Conference Center in New York state. Today, a variation of one of the beautifully crafted lampposts found on the grounds of the inn is incorporated as part of the hotel's logo with "The Dearborn Inn" found in script. Marriott International currently manages Dearborn Inn.

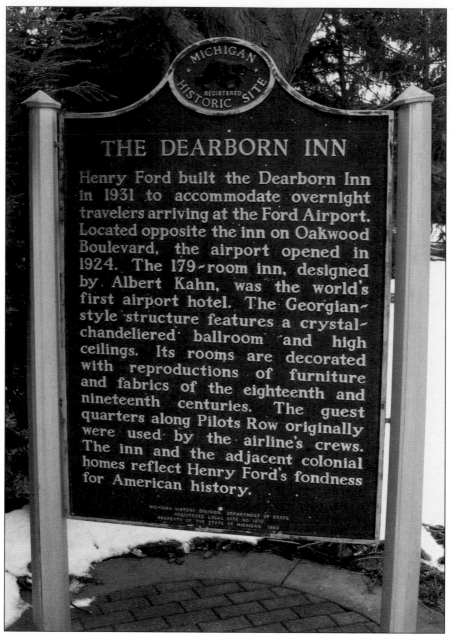

Located at Dearborn Inn, this Michigan State Historic Site Marker (No. 1070) states: "Henry Ford built the Dearborn Inn in 1931 to accommodate overnight travelers arriving at the Ford Airport. Located opposite the inn on Oakwood Boulevard, the airport opened in 1924. The 179-room inn, designed by Albert Kahn, was the world's first airport hotel. The Georgian-style structure features a crystal-chandeliered ballroom and high ceilings. Its rooms are decorated with reproductions of furniture and fabrics of the 18th and 19th centuries. The guest quarters along Pilots Row originally were used by the airline's crews. The inn and adjacent colonial homes reflect Henry Ford's fondness for American history." Note that when the hotel opened in 1931, it possessed 108 rooms. Later documentation has also shown Dearborn Inn to be amongst other airport hotels built during the earliest years of commercial aviation.

When the dedication of the Wright Brother Home and Cycle Shop took place at Greenfield Village, a dinner was held at Dearborn Inn. Henry Ford (left) is seated at the head table with the guest of honor, Orville Wright. (Courtesy of Walter P. Reuther Library, Wayne State University.)

In October 1934, Dr. Piccard and his wife, Jeannette, were photographed here at Dearborn Inn before piloting a balloon on a stratospheric flight. They ascended from the Ford Airport and ended in Cadiz, Ohio, having reached an altitude of 10.98 miles. Jeannette Piccard maintained control of the balloon for its entire record-breaking flight. She was the first licensed female balloon pilot in the United States and the first woman to enter the stratosphere.

Many celebrities and prominent guests have come through the front doors of Dearborn Inn. Shown here is general manager Adrian A. deVogel greeting Lassie upon the dog's arrival to the hotel with a friendly "shake of the paw." The well-known canine was in Michigan to promote a dog food product. (Courtesy of Adrian A. deVogel.)

General manager Adrian A. deVogel graciously produced the inn's guest registry and placed it on a coffee table in the hotel lobby for Lassie to sign in. At the time this famous dog placed a paw in the book, it had already been signed by Henry and Clara Ford, Edsel Ford, Orville Wright, Eleanor Roosevelt, Norman Rockwell, Walt Disney, and many other noted dignitaries. (Courtesy of Adrian A. deVogel.)

If visiting Dearborn Inn and leaving celebrity photographs for the staff was not enough, Lassie also left a "Best Wishes" when pressing a paw-print into the guest registry. (Courtesy of Dearborn Inn.)

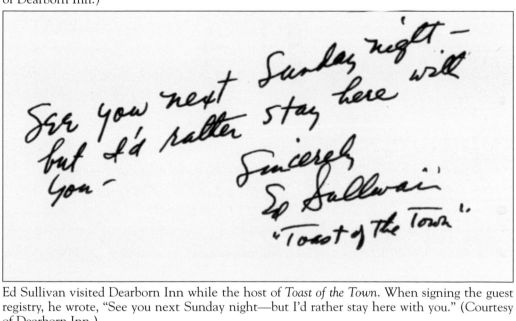

Ed Sullivan visited Dearborn Inn while the host of *Toast of the Town*. When signing the guest registry, he wrote, "See you next Sunday night—but I'd rather stay here with you." (Courtesy of Dearborn Inn.)

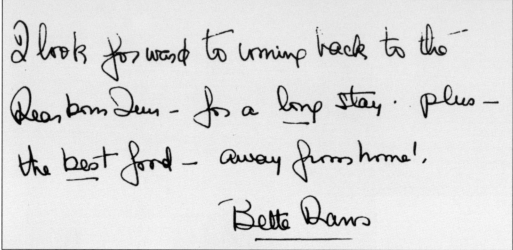

Bette Davis was not the first visitor to notice what amazing meals were served at Dearborn Inn. In the guest registry she notes, "I look forward to coming back to the Dearborn Inn—for a <u>long</u> stay, plus—the <u>best</u> food—away from home!" When Duncan Hines visited, he documented his thoughts by writing, "This is my favorite Inn." (Courtesy of Dearborn Inn.)

When Edgar Bergen visited Dearborn Inn, he left behind something very special in the guest registry besides his own signature—a sketch of Charlie McCarthy and Mortimer Snerd. (Courtesy of Dearborn Inn.)

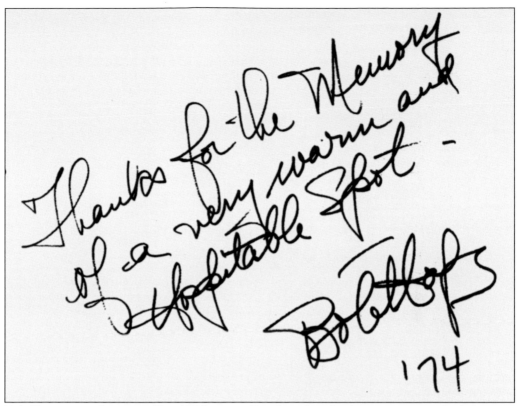

Bob Hope certainly enjoyed his 1974 visit to Dearborn Inn. In the guest registry, he left a note reading, "Thanks for the Memory of a very warm and Hospitable Spot." Other famous signatures in the guest registry include pilot William Stout, first lady Mrs. Woodrow Wilson, artist Diego Rivera, architect Albert Kahn, actor Jimmy Stewart, columnist Ann Landers, and Olympic skater Peggy Flemings. (Courtesy of Dearborn Inn.)

With unsurprising flair, Liberace sketched a grand piano in the guest registry with the following heartfelt message, "Thank you for a wonderful experience in reliving American History at the Museum & Village and topped off by a wonderful dinner—American style!" The last signatures placed in the amazing Dearborn Inn guest registry were of Vice President George Bush and Barbara Bush on October 14, 1987. They wrote, "Thank you for your great hospitality—a very special place with very special people." The hotel would soon close for renovations, and the guest registry would be placed in the care of the Benson Ford Research Center at The Henry Ford. (Courtesy of Dearborn Inn.)

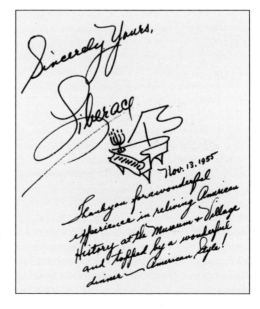

In 1966, a family of four could reserve a room at the Dearborn Inn Motor House for under $25 per night. Rollaway beds were an additional $2; cribs were free. Michigan sales tax was still four percent at this time, and Richard D. McLain was serving as the general manager. (Courtesy of Henry Ford Centennial Library.)

In 1966, Dearborn Inn's reservation request form proudly displayed the AAA emblem and indicated that the hotel was a Master Hosts establishment. This card was preprinted with dates for an upcoming Wedgwood International Seminar taking place at the hotel. Well before the Internet was established and online reservations became the norm, this small card is a flashback to how business was conducted . . . on paper. (Courtesy of Henry Ford Centennial Library.)

The sign on the side of this late-1950s vehicle states, "Staff Car Courtesy Lincoln Division Ford Motors." Here, general manager Adrian A. deVogel (in the suit) greets the "Outstanding Airman of the Year" outside the front of the inn. (Courtesy of Adrian A. deVogel.)

The Dearborn Inn

DINNER

$3.25

Choice of One

Chopped Chicken Livers *40*   Orange, Grapefruit and Apple Cup *40*
V-8 Vegetable Juice *25*
Consomme en Tasse Chiffonade *30*   Puree of Green Pea Soup au Crouton *30*

Celery Hearts   Italian Peperoncini   Carrot Curls

Fried Combination Seafood Plate, Cole Slaw, Tartar Sauce *260*
Broiled Fresh Whitefish from the Great Lakes, Parsley Butter Sauce *250*
Julienne of Chicken, Mushrooms a la King in Crisp, Pattie Shell *270*
Pan Fried Smoked Ham Steak, Country Gravy, Pineapple Ring *270*
Mignonette of Beef Tenderloin off the Griddle, Bordelaise Sauce *300*

CHEF LeVEQUE'S SUGGESTIONS
Broiled Fresh Ocean Swordfish Steak, Maitre D'Hotel *245*
Sweetbreads Saute, Grilled Ham on Crouton, Fresh Mushrooms *280*

Choice of Two

Lyonnaise Potatoes   Au Gratin Potatoes
Fresh Mixed Vegetables   Whole Kernel Corn in Butter

Limestone Lettuce Salad *30* or   Jellied Fruit Salad, Cream Dressing *30*
French, Mayonnaise, or Thousand Island Dressing

Rhubarb Pie *30*   Strawberry Tapioca Pudding *30*   Two Tone Layer Cake *30*
Fruit Jello *25*   Blueberry Cream Tartlette *30*   Bleu Cheese *35*
Burnt Almond Ice Cream *40*   Brandied Peach Sundae *50*   Sherbet *30*
(All Pastry, Cakes, Pies and Rolls baked in our own Bakery)

Broiled Prime Sirloin Steak
With
Choice of All Items From Regular Menu
$5.00

Coffee   Tea   Milk   Buttermilk   Chocolate Milk

Tuesday, March 10, 1953

Many talented and hardworking chefs and assistants have staffed the kitchen of Dearborn Inn over the past 80 years. Chef Paul LeVeque cooked for Henry and Clara Ford and worked at the inn for more than 30 years. This dinner menu from Tuesday, March 10, 1953, lists "Broiled Fresh Ocean Swordfish Steak" as chef LeVeque's suggestion, priced at just $2.45. Chef LeVeque worked six days a week and kept a room at the inn, where he could sleep for a few hours midday between starting an early shift and working late into the evenings. (From the family collection of chef Paul LeVeque.)

116

The food at Dearborn Inn seems to have always been an attraction, and a June 11, 1964, headline and photograph in the *Dearborn Press* stated, "Dearborn Inn Features Includes Special Buffets." Boasting several awards, the article went on to describe, "Special features of the Inn include a men's buffet luncheon on weekdays and a Seafood Fantasy on Friday nights. The Sunday afternoon brunches are extremely popular as are the Sunday evening buffet suppers." An appetizer on this menu lists mushroom caps stuffed with crabmeat au gratin, priced at $2.25. (From the family collection of chef Paul LcVeque.)

The Dearborn Inn

Appetizers

While You Are Having Your Cocktail Enjoy	
Hot or Cold Appetizer Assortment for 2	3.35
Mushroom Caps Stuffed	Holland Herring 1.60
w/Crabmeat Au Gratin 2.25	Onion Rings, Sour Cream
Iced Gulf Shrimp Cocktail 2.50	French Onion Soup Gratinee ...... .90
Soup du Jour ...... .60	

The Inn's Salad Buffet

We invite you to prepare your own relish and salad plate.
If you wish, your waitress will be happy to prepare it for you.

WELCOME

Wayfarers and Local Gentry

The Caterer will be happy to consult with you concerning special chambers for merrymaking and festivities and assembly rooms where gentlemen of commerce may gather in private.

A 1964 *Dearborn Press* article stated, "Businessmen are finding the atmosphere at the inn a very relaxing and informal one. One group of salesmen held their meeting under a shady tree by the pool with lunch and dinner served cook-out style." A section of the inn's menu contained the following information: "Welcome Wayfarers and Local Gentry. The Caterer will be happy to consult with you concerning special chambers for merrymaking and festivities and assembly rooms where gentlemen of commerce may gather in private." (From the family collection of chef Paul LeVeque.)

Woodchuck Hash

(updated version of the 1850 recipe)
  3/4 lb cooked pork sausage
  1/2 lb bacon, cooked
  2 1/2 lb cooked, leftover beef
  1 large onion, chopped
  4 stalks celery
  1 1/2 cups brown sauce
  3 cloves garlic, chopped
  5 cups mashed potatoes or
    garlic mashed potatoes

Grind first five ingredients in a meat grinder. Heat a large sauté pan and mix all ingredients, except mashed potatoes, and warm through completely. Add a touch of water if necessary, then skin as much fat off the top as possible. Place in 8 to 10 individual casserole dishes or one large serving dish, and pipe mashed potatoes on top. Brown in oven. Serve immediately with a fresh salad and bread. Makes 8 to 10 portions.

In March 1994, Nancy Kennedy included this recipe from the Dearborn Inn's Ten Eyck Tavern restaurant in her *Ford World* newspaper article. The recipe was based on a 1850s dish served by Conrad Ten Eyck. Ten Eyck was an early Dearborn innkeeper who operated a stagecoach stop located between Detroit and Chicago along a plank road that is now known as Michigan Avenue (US 12).

When Queen Juliana of the Netherlands visited Dearborn Inn in 1952, manager Robert E. Hamilton and catering manager Steve Ronce thoroughly investigated proper procedures for royal entertaining etiquette. Clara Cook included this recipe from chef LeVeque in her article for the *Detroit News* with the headline "Chef Shares 'Dish to Set Before a Queen' With News Readers."

ROYAL SQUAB WINDSOR

Soak in cold water one hour, wash and drain:
  1 cup rice
Combine:
  chopped livers from squab
  2 mushroom caps, chopped
  1 shallot, chopped fine
  1 teaspoons raw ham, chopped
  ½ teaspoon parsley
Sauté in butter, but do not let brown, add rice. Cook, stirring on top of stove for 5 minutes. Stuff boned squabs with rice mixture. Add to cover:
  chicken broth
Bake in oven at 325 degrees for 20 to 25 minutes.
Add for each squab:
  small carrot
  small onion
  branch of celery
  small glass of white wine
When squab is done remove. Place roasting pan on stove and cook to reduce juice. Add teaspoon of meat glaze; season and strain. Pour over squab to serve or serve in dish at side.
  * * *

*The Management
and Staff of
The Dearborn Inn
cordially invite you to share in the
celebration of our
Fiftieth Anniversary,
Wednesday, the first of July,
nineteen hundred and eighty one.
Reception 5:30 to 8:00 in the evening
at the Dearborn Inn*

*Please present invitation
upon arrival*

Fifty years after Henry, Clara, and Edsel Ford opened the doors of Dearborn Inn, a celebration equal to the opening reception was being planned. In keeping with the formality of the original invitations sent to guests announcing the opening of the inn in 1931, printed invitations were mailed out for the 50th anniversary and stated: "The Management and Staff of The Dearborn Inn cordially invite you to share in the celebration of our Fiftieth Anniversary, Wednesday, the first of July, nineteen hundred and eighty one. Reception 5:30 to 8:00 in the evening at the Dearborn Inn. Please present invitation upon arrival." (Courtesy of Adrian A. deVogel.)

MENU

WELCOME Jimmy Launce - WJR Radio	Cocktails	Hors d'Oeuvres Variés
		∙∙∙
Introduction of Special Guests		Potage Crème de Vichysoisse Allumettes au Fromage
		∙∙∙
Invocation Reverend Richard J. Knaus	Piesporter Goldtröpfchen 1976	Filet de Soles a la Florentine Sauce Nantua fleurs de Broccoli - Sauce Hollandaise
		∙∙∙
∙∙∙		Salade Composée aux légumes - Sauce Maitre Cuisine
		∙∙∙
DINNER	Sonoma Rosé of Cabernet 1977	Tendron de Veau grillée - Sauce Marsala Nouilles à la lyonnaise Asperges Verts au beurre
∙∙∙		∙∙∙
Program		fromage Brie avec fruits fraiche Biscuits Americaine
Remarks Adrian deVogel Vice President & General Manager	Sandeman's Fine Vintage Port	∙∙∙ Pâtisserie "Dearborn Inn 50"
		∙∙∙
	Liqueurs	Café
		Maître d'Hôtel - Liam O'Brien Chef de Cuisine - George Riley

To Ans deVogel:
From her friend and admirer.
J. H. Doolittle

The 50th anniversary celebration took place in the Alexandria Ballroom, and guests received a copy of the program and dinner menu, including a list of wines to be served. Jimmy Launce of Detroit's WJR radio presented the opening remarks, and pilot Jimmy Doolittle was one of many special guests. Ans deVogel, wife of general manager Adrian A. deVogel, had her program autographed by Doolittle. The maître d'hôtel was Liam O'Brien, and the chef de cuisine was George Riley. (Courtesy of Ans deVogel.)

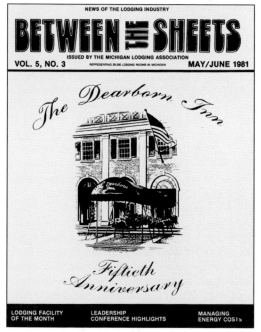

Between the Sheets magazine, issued by the Michigan Lodging Association, featured Dearborn Inn on the cover of its May/June 1981 issue, highlighting the 50th anniversary of the hotel. (Courtesy of Adrian A. deVogel.)

Many individuals enjoyed long careers working at Dearborn Inn. When vice president and general manager Adrian A. "Dutch" deVogel retired in 1985, he received this note from William Clay Ford. "Your cooperation over the years . . . is deeply appreciated by my family and myself," Ford wrote. Other inn employees also received hand-written holiday cards and notes from members of the Ford family throughout the years, illustrating the importance of the inn to subsequent generations of the Ford family and their appreciation for those who served as caretakers. (Courtesy of Adrian A. deVogel.)

William Clay Ford
P. O. Box 1800
Dearborn, Michigan 48121-1800

December 27, 1985

Mr. Adrian A. deVogel

Dear Dutch:

Although I am unable to be present at the celebration of your retirement this evening, I join everyone else in the tribute to your thirty years of loyal and distinguished service to The Dearborn Inn.

Your long career at the Inn has spanned many changes, and it should be a source of pride that you have been a leader in its continued growth and development. Your cooperation over the years, both with The Edison Institute and Ford Motor Company, is deeply appreciated by my family and myself.

You have done an outstanding job, Dutch, and I hope you will carry with you many fond memories of your association with The Dearborn Inn.

Best wishes for a healthy, happy retirement.

Sincerely,

Bill Ford

William Clay Ford

As chairman of the Edison Institute and of Seaboard Properties, William Clay Ford appointed Adrian A. deVogel the new general manager of Dearborn Inn, to succeed Richard McLain, in 1971. DeVogel had served in several other capacities at the hotel and restaurant since 1955. After extending 30 years of hospitality to visitors at Dearborn Inn, Dutch deVogel and his wife, Ans, are pictured here celebrating his retirement with friends, family, staff, and the community. (Courtesy of Adrian A. deVogel.)

This Ford Motor Company press-release photograph shows an aerial view from the rear of the hotel during the renovation of the inn in the late 1980s. J.M. Olson Corporation handled the project on behalf of Ford Land, with Nordstrom-Samson serving as the architect. The three Colonial cottages toward the right of the image—Fritchie, Whitman, and Poe—were relocated during the renovation to align the five historic homes in a gentle arching arrangement behind the hotel, making space for the hotel's new addition. Tara B. Gnau wrote in *The Dearborn Historian* that Charles Hart, the architect for Treadway Inns who designed the cottages in the 1930s, "felt that since many of the Dearborn Inn's guests were visitors to the Edison Institute [Henry Ford Museum and Greenfield Village] they should have the opportunity to stay in an environment much like the ones they had visited." (Courtesy of Henry Ford Centennial Library.)

In July 2006, Dearborn Inn again celebrated a major anniversary, having now served the community and guests for 75 years. An open house with guided tours allowed attendees to stroll through the hotel and visit each of the five cottages, while a classic auto show took place on the lush front lawn. Over 2,000 guests came to celebrate and enjoy a grand ice cream social, complete with a barbershop quartet for entertainment.

The sun porch provides a beautiful view of the courtyard and well-maintained gardens, as well as a glimpse of the historic cottages set behind the hotel. At one time, the sun porch was the location of the Serendipity Shop, which served as the hotel's gift shop. Today, the sun porch is still an ideal place to meet friends, read a book, or sit and relax while enjoying the cheerful and comfortable surroundings. (Courtesy of Dearborn Inn.)

Today, an American flag continues to be flown from the upper-floor window of the Barbara Fritchie House in honor of the patriot. Great detail was put into finding actual measurements and records to make the five historic cottage reproductions as accurate as possible, and all remain available for guests when staying at Dearborn Inn.

Significant investments and updates to Dearborn Inn continue to take place. The Early American Room has undergone transformation and is known as Edison's today. The popular restaurant serves breakfast, lunch, and dinner to guests and visitors, who can still enjoy a splendid view out the large, arched windows. (Courtesy of Dearborn Inn.)

The stately beauty of the main lobby is as breathtaking as when the inn first opened. Comfortable seating and exquisite architectural details make it worthwhile to arrive at the Dearborn Inn a few minutes early to sit and enjoy the ambiance of the space. (Courtesy of Dearborn Inn.)

The Ten Eyck Tavern now serves as the inn's signature bar, with comfortable seating in a relaxed environment. Amenities include flat-panel, high-definition televisions and wireless Internet access. (Courtesy of Dearborn Inn.)

Still as stunning as when Henry and Clara Ford hosted dances here, the Alexandria Ballroom maintains its original charm and elegantly appointed details. This space continues to serve wedding receptions, meetings, and other gatherings as one of several ballrooms that comprise over 17,000 square feet of banquet space now available at Dearborn Inn. (Courtesy of Dearborn Inn.)

Since 1931, Dearborn Inn has graced its namesake city, sitting quietly away from Oakwood Boulevard and greeting visitors on its wide semicircular driveway. Still beautifully landscaped and surrounded by its signature lampposts, a step through the front door is like a step back in time—without losing a touch of today's modern conveniences. Henry Ford's vision of a modern hostelry has been through many transitions, but its traditional excellence continues to be preserved for all to enjoy.

BIBLIOGRAPHY

Bryan, Ford R. *The Fords of Dearborn*. Detroit: Harlo Press, 1987.

Clark, Barbara L. "A Modern Hotel's Colonial Village." *American Home*. May 1940: 59–112.

Fox, Jean M. *More Than a Tavern: 150 Years of Botsford Inn*. Farmington Hills, MI: Farmington Hills Historical Commission, 1986.

Gnau, Tara B. "Decorative Dancing and Damask Dining." *The Dearborn Historian*. Summer 1981: 65–75.

Hotel Monthly. "Historic Village to House Dearborn Inn Enlargement." April 1937: 24–29.

Larkins, Ronald T. Reuther and William T. *Oakland Aviation*. Charleston, SC: Arcadia Publishing, 2008.

Lewis, David L. "Dearborn Inn." *Ford Life*. November/December 1972: 25–28.

———. *The Public Image of Henry Ford*. Detroit: Wayne State University Press, 1976.

Marsdale, James. "The Dearborn Inn: Scrupulous Cleanliness in the Dominating Factor." *Building Maintenance*. May 1932.

O'Callaghan, Timothy J. *The Aviation Legacy of Henry & Edsel Ford*. Ann Arbor: Proctor Publications, LLC, 2000.

Talcott, Richard Bennett. "Dearborn Inn." *The Letter Booklet*. Boston: Richard Bennett Talcott, 1951.

The Dearbornite. "Henry Ford Builds a Modern Hotel." September 1930: 25.

Twork, Eva O'Neal. *Henry Ford and Benjamin B. Lovett*. Detroit: Harlo Press, 1982.

Upward, Geoffrey C. *A Home for Our Heritage*. Dearborn, MI: The Henry Ford Museum Press, 1979.

www.arcadiapublishing.com

Discover books about the town where you grew up, the cities where your friends and families live, the town where your parents met, or even that retirement spot you've been dreaming about. Our Web site provides history lovers with exclusive deals, advanced notification about new titles, e-mail alerts of author events, and much more.

Find Your Place in History.